P9-CFJ-035

50 Early Childhood Guidance Strategies

JANICE J. BEATY

Elmira College, Emerita

TOURO COLLEGE LIBRARY
Kings Hwy

WITHDRAWN

PEARSON

Merrill
Prentice Hall

Upper Saddle River, New Jersey
Columbus, Ohio

KH

Library of Congress Cataloging in Publication Data

Vice President and Executive Publisher: Jeffery W. Johnston
Publisher: Kevin M. Davis
Editor: Julie Peters
Editorial Assistant: Michelle Girgis
Production Editor: Sheryl Glicker Langner
Design Coordinator: Diane C. Lorenzo
Cover Design: Ali Mohrman
Cover Image: Getty One
Production Manager: Laura Messerly
Director of Marketing: Ann Castel Davis
Marketing Manager: Autumn Purdy
Marketing Coordinator: Amy Judd

This book was set in Optima by Carlisle Communications, Ltd. It was printed and bound by Banta Book Group.
The cover was printed by Phoenix Color Corp.

Photo Credits: All photos courtesy of Janice Beaty.

Copyright © 2006 by Pearson Education, Inc., Upper Saddle River, New Jersey 07458. Pearson Prentice Hall.
All rights reserved. Printed in the United States of America. This publication is protected by Copyright and
permission should be obtained from the publisher prior to any prohibited reproduction, storage in a retrieval
system, or transmission in any form or by any means, electronic, mechanical, photocopying, recording, or
likewise. For information regarding permission(s), write to: Rights and Permissions Department.

Pearson Prentice Hall™ is a trademark of Pearson Education, Inc.
Pearson® is a registered trademark of Pearson plc
Prentice Hall® is a registered trademark of Pearson Education, Inc.
Merrill® is a registered trademark of Pearson Education, Inc.

Pearson Education Ltd.
Pearson Education Singapore Pte. Ltd.
Pearson Education Canada, Ltd.
Pearson Education–Japan

Pearson Education Australia Pty. Limited
Pearson Education North Asia Ltd.
Pearson Educación de Mexico, S.A. de C.V.
Pearson Education Malaysia Pte. Ltd.

PEARSON
Merrill
Prentice Hall

10 9 8 7 6 5 4 3 2 1
ISBN: 0-13-170014-6

11/21/06

Preface

An early childhood classroom can be a most exciting adventure for teachers, student teachers, and volunteers who come prepared to interact with today's exuberant, inquisitive, and eager young children. But what about the children who act too rowdy, or take others' toys, or can't seem to get along with anyone? How will you deal with disruptive children without resorting to harsh words or punishment? *Fifty Early Childhood Guidance Strategies* has an answer in its easy-to-use, easy-to understand approach involving young children's own emerging prosocial behaviors.

You will learn how children come to act the way they do and how you can help them convert inappropriate behavior to constructive outcomes by using positive guidance. Positive guidance assists you in becoming calmly involved on a one-to-one basis with children exhibiting inappropriate behavior. You will learn how to assess such behavior, how to redirect it, and how to get children involved in controlling their actions.

This text takes advantage of the latest child development research by presenting strategies that speak to the way children learn. These strategies are tied to the ordinary contents and activities of an early childhood classroom, including blocks, books, sand and water play, dramatic play, puppets, finger painting, easel painting, scissors, and songs.

Each strategy begins with a guidance concept that briefly but concisely explains the topic. Next come steps you can use in applying positive guidance in instances where children are involved in attention-seeking, group entry conflicts, possession conflicts, power struggles, or other inappropriate behavior. You learn to handle these behaviors through coaching children on how to act, modeling acceptable behavior, using nonverbal cues, and demonstrating your acceptance of every child. Children learn to handle these behaviors through being allowed to express their feelings in words, painting, water play, puppet play, appropriate story re-enactments, and games. There are more than 50 ways.

Each child comes into your classroom as a unique individual with a background different from every other child. Most can't wait to become involved in the exciting plethora of toys and equipment they see before them. Most don't notice there are all those other children with the same thing on their minds. Will they collide with one another or cooperate? Will there be smiles or crying before it is over? You can be the one who sets the tone with your own smiling face, knowing you have a tool box full of 50 conflict-converting, harmony-constructing tools at your beck and call ready to go to work. Just open the book and get started.

KEY FEATURES

- Strategies are arranged alphabetically for easy selection. On the inside front cover is a table of the strategies grouped by category.

- Many of the strategies are tied to children's picture books at the early childhood level. More than 150 of the finest books have been selected and described or listed within the strategies.

- The activities described have been chosen as models for your easy use, as well as to emulate with your own ideas.

- Assessment of children's appropriate behavior progress can be partially accomplished with the following checklists: Sharing Behavior, Early Childhood Behavior, Group Entry Strategies, Child-Centered Learning Centers, and Self-Esteem.

USING THIS BOOK

Fifty Early Childhood Guidance Strategies can be used by itself as a handy activities book by teachers, student teachers, and volunteers. It can also be used in any early childhood methods and materials course or guidance course. College students especially appreciate activity books like this for use in their student teaching or practicum experiences. In addition it can be used as a supplement to guidance textbooks such as the author's *Prosocial Guidance for the Preschool Child*, or other textbooks by the author such as *Skills for Preschool Teachers* and *Observing Development of the Young Child*. The author has also published *50 Early Childhood Literacy Strategies* with Merrill Education/Prentice Hall.

ACKNOWLEDGMENTS

The author wishes to thank her editor Julie Peters for her encouragement and support; Ann Gilchrist, director of the Central Missouri Foster Grandparents program, for allowing me to work with and film the wonderful grandparents working in Head Start programs in central Missouri; Sheryl Langner, production editor, for her special talent in making textbooks attractave; and for the following programs and parents for allowing me to photograph their children: Park Avenue and Fay Street Head Starts in Columbia and Fulton, Missouri; Williams Family Center Head Start and Almost Home Day Care in Mexico, Missouri; Walnut Creek Day School, Columbia, Missouri; Noah's Ark Preschool in Taos, New Mexico; and Arnot Museum Nursery School in Elmira, New York. Also I wish to thank Elaine West, executive director of the Missouri Association for Community Action, for allowing me to use some of the exciting calendar art for the MACA calendar. Thanks to the young artists and their teachers and parents from Head Starts in Mt. Vernon, Park Hills, Poplar Bluff, Portageville, Springfield, St. Joseph, Steele, University City and Warsaw, Missouri.

DISCOVER THE COMPANION WEBSITE ACCOMPANYING THIS BOOK

THE PRENTICE HALL COMPANION WEBSITE: A VIRTUAL LEARNING ENVIRONMENT

Technology is a constantly growing and changing aspect of our field that is creating a need for content and resources. To address this emerging need, Prentice Hall has developed an online learning environment for students and professors alike—Companion Websites—to support our textbooks.

In creating a Companion Website, our goal is to build on and enhance what the textbook already offers. For this reason, the content for each user-friendly website is organized by chapter and provides the professor and student with a variety of meaningful resources. Common features of a Companion Website include:

FOR THE PROFESSOR

Every Companion Website integrates Syllabus Manager™, an online syllabus creation and management utility.

- **Syllabus Manager™** provides you, the instructor, with an easy, step-by-step process to create and revise syllabi, with direct links into Companion Website and other online content without having to learn HTML.
- Students may logon to your syllabus during any study session. All they need to know is the web address for the Companion Website and the password you've assigned to your syllabus.
- After you have created a syllabus using **Syllabus Manager™,** students may enter the syllabus for their course section from any point in the Companion Website.
- Class dates are highlighted in white and assignment due dates appear in blue. Clicking on a date, the student is shown the list of activities for the assignment. The activities for each assignment are linked directly to actual content, saving time for students.
- Adding assignments consists of clicking on the desired due date, then filling in the details of the assignment—name of the assignment, instructions, and whether or not it is a one-time or repeating assignment.

- In addition, links to other activities can be created easily. If the activity is online, a URL can be entered in the space provided, and it will be linked automatically in the final syllabus.
- Your completed syllabus is hosted on our servers, allowing convenient updates from any computer on the Internet. Changes you make to your syllabus are immediately available to your students at their next logon.

FOR THE STUDENT

- **Chapter Objectives**—outline key concepts from the text
- **Projects**—allow students to become familiar with conducting research on the Web. Self-assessment quizzes are often linked to chapter projects and text applications or guidelines
- **Interactive Self-quizzes**—complete with hints and automatic grading that provide i mediate feedback for students. After students submit their answers for the interactive self-quizzes, the Companion Website Results Reporter computes a percentage grade, provides a graphic representation of how many questions were answered correctly and incorrectly, and gives a question-by-question analysis of the quiz. Students are given the option to send their quiz to up to four email addresses (professor, teaching assistant, study partner, etc.).
- **Message Board**—serves as a virtual bulletin board to post—or respond to—questions or comments to/from a national audience
- **Net Searches**—offer links by key terms from each chapter to related Internet content
- **Web Destinations**—links to www sites that relate to chapter content
- **Additional Resources**—access to chapter-specific or general content that enhances material found in the text

To take advantage of these and other resources, please visit the Practical Research: Planning and Design Companion Website at

www.prenhall.com/leedy

EDUCATOR LEARNING CENTER: AN INVALUABLE ONLINE RESOURCE

Merrill Education and the Association for Supervision and Curriculum Development (ASCD) invite you to take advantage of a new online resource, one that provides access to the top research and proven strategies associated with ASCD and Merrill—the Educator Learning Center. At **www.educatorlearningcenter.com**, you will find resources that will enhance your students' understanding of course topics and of current educational issues, in addition to being invaluable for further research.

HOW THE EDUCATOR LEARNING CENTER WILL HELP YOUR STUDENTS BECOME BETTER TEACHERS

With the combined resources of Merrill Education and ASCD, you and your students will find a wealth of tools and materials to better prepare them for the classroom.

Research

- More than 600 articles from the ASCD journal Educational Leadership discuss everyday issues faced by practicing teachers.
- A direct link on the site to Research Navigator™ gives students access to many of the leading education journals, as well as extensive content detailing the research process.
- Excerpts from Merrill Education texts give your students insights on important topics of instructional methods, diverse populations, assessment, classroom management, technology, and refining classroom practice.

Classroom Practice

- Hundreds of lesson plans and teaching strategies are categorized by content area and age range.
- Case studies and classroom video footage provide virtual field experience for student reflection.
- Computer simulations and other electronic tools keep your students abreast of today's classrooms and current technologies.

LOOK INTO THE VALUE OF EDUCATOR LEARNING CENTER YOURSELF

A four-month subscription to Educator Learning Center is $25 but is FREE when packaged with any Merrill Education text. In order for your students to have access to this site, you must use this special value-pack ISBN number WHEN placing your textbook order with the bookstore: 013-1862081. Your students will then receive a copy of the text packaged with a free ASCD pincode. To preview the value of this website to you and your students, please go to www.educatorlearningcenter.com and click on "Demo."

Contents

Chapter Index of Children's Picture Books
(Listed or Described)

(*multicultural)

1

ASSESSING BEHAVIOR

CONCEPT

For young children 3-to-5 years old, action is the name of the game. Most of them are always on the go, or so it seems. Where do they get all their energy? Won't they ever slow down? Oh-oh! Shawn bumps into Gregory and down they both go. Now there are tears and accusations: "It's his fault! He did it!" "I didn't do anything! He was in the way! Crybaby!" And so it goes.

What is a teacher, student teacher, or volunteer to do in a classroom of 15-to-20 youngsters who never seem to stop? How do you get them to calm down? How do you help them to work and play peacefully? Isn't there some magic wand you can wave over them to make them behave?

Yes, there is. It is called "positive guidance," and not "discipline." The adults who learn to use positive guidance in an early childhood classroom can truly become child behavior magicians. It may not be easy at first. It may not work in the blink of an eye like your angry voice exclaiming: "Get up, Shawn! Now look what you've done! Can't you ever watch where you're going?" Or: "It's time-out for you, Shawn! How many times have I told you not to run in the classroom? Go sit in the time-out chair!" But if you learn how to use positive guidance with young children, it will not only decrease behavior problems, it will prevent them from happening over and over.

This text has been designed to help you become a child behavior magician by using some of the 50 guidance strategies described, and not using negative discipline or punishment when inappropriate behavior strikes. Positive guidance implies becoming calmly involved on a one-to-one basis with the children involved in such behavior. It is based on your knowledge of child behavior: how to assess it; how to redirect it; and how to get the children involved in controlling their own inappropriate behavior (see chapter 17: Guidance). How do you do this?

First of all, you need to assess the behavior of each child over a period of time. You will be establishing a behavior benchmark for each one, helping you to know how to proceed from there. Is the child a smiler or straight-faced? Loud-voiced or silent? Does she make friends easily or keep to herself? Will he share with others or defend his property with force? As you assess each child's behavior and establish his or her personal benchmark, you will be guided to the particular strategies that work best with that child. In other words, not every guidance strategy works the same with every individual.

Behavior assessment of young children is accomplished through systematic observing and recording using an instrument that focuses on particular behavior. The focus should be on *appropriate* child behavior and not *inappropriate* behavior. The guidance strategies you use will also focus on appropriate behavior. What will you look for? You can make your own behavior checklist or use one of the observation checklists included in this text.

STEPS

1. **Make a behavior observation checklist.**
2. **Use a behavior observation checklist to observe and record.**
3. **Use the checklist results to plan activities for the child.**

ACTIVITIES

1. **Make a behavior observation checklist.**
   - Make a general list of the kinds of behaviors you want to assess. Such a list might include: communicating, helpfulness, movement, sharing, or turn-taking.
   - Select one of these topics (all are strategies in this text) and list under it all of the behaviors pertaining to it you can think of, both appropriate and inappropriate. For example, for "sharing" you might list:

does not share	takes toys from others
does not understand sharing	keeps own possessions
cries if made to share	shares without a fuss

   - Choose about four of these behaviors that are most important to you and rewrite them as *appropriate* behaviors in a checklist format. For example: for sharing you might include the behaviors shown in Figure 1–1.

2. **Use a behavior observation checklist to observe and record.**
   - Select the child to observe and set up a time with the other staff members when you will be observing. Choose times when the child is playing with others using toys.
   - Be as unobtrusive as possible so children will not notice. Try not to make eye contact with the child. If you do, turn away quickly. If other children ask what you are doing, say you're making a list and ask if they would also like to make a list in the writing center. (Have materials available.)
   - Check off what you see happening. Your checklist should contain space for you to write comments on what you see happening. If you do not check an item, you should indicate why. Periodically continue observing and recording until you get a complete picture.

3. **Use the checklist results to plan activities for the child.**
   - Use the checklist results to determine what the child's strengths are (checked items) and what his needs are (blanks). Use his strengths to help him accomplish his needs. Needs are not weaknesses; they are areas that need strengthening.
   - Share checklist results with the staff and set up activities to help the child learn to share (see chapter 40: Sharing).
   - Help the child feel good every time he shares by thanking him for doing it.
   - Such a short checklist can be part of a longer, more complete behavior checklist for a child. If you make one yourself, choose other behaviors you want to look for and add them to this first one, always focusing on the positive accomplishments of each child. Remember, checklist items should be positive. Inappropriate behavior is indicated by the blanks, the items you do not check. Thus, your own focus will also be positive: what's right with a child, not what's wrong.
   - You may prefer to use the Early Childhood Behavior Checklist included as Figure 1–2. If certain items show up as blanks, you may want to expand those particular items to show

FIGURE 1–1 Sharing Behaviors Checklist.

```
Name _____  Observer _____

_____ Understands what sharing is about

_____ Shares toys and materials without a fuss

_____ Lets another child use his/her possessions

_____ Asks another child to share his/her toy
```

Name _____ Age _____ Observer _____

1. *Attention-seeking*
   ____ Does not seek adult attention
   ____ Finds others to play with

2. *Attention-span*
   ____ Stays with an activity to completion
   ____ Does not wander from activity to activity

3. *Behavior control*
   ____ Controls own behavior
   ____ Stays within behavior limits

4. *Conflicts*
   ____ Resolves conflicts peaceably
   ____ Avoids conflict situations

5. *Feelings*
   ____ Expresses feelings in words
   ____ Allows strong feelings to be redirected

6. *Friends*
   ____ Makes friends easily
   ____ Seeks others to play with

7. *Helping, cooperating*
   ____ Picks up materials without a fuss
   ____ Complies with adult requests

8. *Limits*
   ____ Follows limits set by others
   ____ Helps to set limits for self

9. *Humor*
   ____ Enjoys humorous stories, situations
   ____ Laughs a lot

10. *Other-esteem*
    ____ Gets along with other children
    ____ Can tell how another child feels

11. *Play Groups*
    ____ Gains access to play groups easily
    ____ Allows others to enter play group

12. *Respect*
    ____ Treats other children's materials respectfully
    ____ Treats children who seem different with respect

13. *Self-esteem*
    ____ Is not afraid of new people or situations
    ____ Smiles, seems happy much of the time

14. *Sharing, turn-taking*
    ____ Shares toys and materials with others
    ____ Takes turns without a fuss

FIGURE 1–2 Early Childhood Behavior Checklist.

Note: The publisher grants permission to reproduce this checklist for evaluation and record keeping.

Teachers can use a checklist to observe how children share.

several other behaviors. Since this checklist includes only two of the most likely behaviors for each item, it gives only an overall, rather than an in-depth, view of a child's behavior. Then go to the *alphabetized strategy name of the item* in this text for ideas and activities to help the child improve.

REFERENCES AND SUGGESTED READINGS

Beaty, J. J. (2006). *Observing development of the young child* (6th ed.). Upper Saddle River, NJ: Merrill/Prentice Hall.

Bentzen, W. R. (2000). *Seeing young children: A guide to observing and recording behavior.* Clifton Park, NY: Thomson Delmar Learning.

Losardo, A., & Notari-Syverson, A. (2001). *Alternative approaches to assessing young children.* Baltimore: Paul H. Brookes.

Marion, M. (2004). *Using observation in early childhood education.* Upper Saddle River, NJ: Merrill/Prentice Hall.

Mindes, G. (2003). *Assessing young children* (2nd ed.). Upper Saddle River, NJ: Merrill/Prentice Hall.

Seefeldt, C. (1998). Assessing young children. In C. Seefeldt & A. Galper (Eds.) *Continuing issues in early childhood education.* Upper Saddle River, NJ: Merrill/Prentice Hall.

2 ATTENTION SPAN

CONCEPT

The short attention span of young children plays an important role in their behavior. The younger the child, the shorter her attention span (i.e, the length of time she will pursue an activity). That is why you see toddlers dashing from one thing to another like busy bees who seldom alight for long on any one activity. It is also why preschool children lose interest easily when circle time drones on and on, or the story being read has a long text on each page. They seem to need constant stimulation with new and exciting materials to keep their attention focused. When their attention wanders they often get restless and begin poking a neighbor or trying to create a diversion.

Some adults blame children's need for this stimulation on their relentless viewing of television with its nonstop flashing of lively images. In reality, attention span has more to do with brain development and, strange as it seems, the infants' interactions with their mothers. Neuroscientists have found that the part of the brain controlling attention is slower to develop than other parts so that younger children have difficulty holding their attention on one thing for long.

On the other hand, other researchers have found that mothers who direct their babies "through talk and gestures, to focus on particular objects, people, and events in their environment, help to determine their later intelligence." "Maternal encouragement of attention" it is called (Eliot, 1999, p. 405).

A child's short attention span does not mean he has the condition known as attention deficit disorder (ADD). This can be diagnosed by a physician only, and most physicians are reluctant to make this diagnosis before a child is 5 or 6 years old. As Nelsen, et al. (1998) note:

> Before that time, impulsive behavior, high activity levels, and short attention spans may be due to temperament or developmental differences. (p. 86)

Because young children's short attention spans cause some children to lose interest in lengthy teacher-directed activities and resort to inappropriate behavior, some teachers have misunderstood how to handle this problem. By constructing brief activity periods to fit short attention spans followed by transitions to the next period, they have unwittingly produced the opposite effect: children's disengagement in learning. When children are disengaged they tend to wander around, often creating disturbances among others. But when children are deeply engaged in their own learning, their attention spans are stretched and their learning increases. Isenberg and Jalongo (1993) have this to say:

> Many teachers erroneously believe that because children have short attention spans, activities must be changed constantly. When young children are engaged in meaningful activities, however, they are capable of concentrating for long periods of time. (p. 176)

If you find your own children becoming disruptive because teacher-directed activities are too long or self-directed activities are too short, here are some suggestions.

STEPS

1. **Give children a choice from a number of interesting new activities.**
2. **Allow children enough time to get deeply involved in the activities.**
3. **Integrate the most successful and longest-lasting activities into every learning center.**

5

ACTIVITIES

1. Give children a choice from a number of interesting new activities.

- Put out several different, more exciting, and intricate puzzles than you have used before. Constructive Playthings (1-800-448-4115) offers giant floor puzzles (24–48 pieces) showing dinosaur scenes and jungle animals, as well as classic story floor puzzles such as *Where the Wild Things Are* and *The Hungry Caterpillar.*

- If children like these, follow up with a large adult-type 100-piece puzzle. Think young children can't complete it? You'll be surprised—if you challenge them and their attention spans! (Put the puzzle on an out-of-the-way table as it may take puzzle-making experts many days to complete.)

- Select an activity that always interests children and set up variations of it in several learning centers on the same day. For instance, water. Have a table with water in a plastic pan in the science center along with a number of wooden, plastic, and metal objects to discover which ones sink or float. Put three muffin tins in the art center, fill their cups with water, put out several little squeeze bottles of liquid food coloring, and challenge children to mix the colors and see what happens. Put several glass jars in the music center, fill them with graduated amounts of water, and challenge children to tap them with spoons to play a tune.

- Obtain some interesting new wooden building block sets for children to use in the block center. Childcraft Education Corporation (1-800-631-5652) offers several new sets of building blocks: skyscraper set, Middle Eastern set (domes and minarets), and Russian set (towers of Moscow and St. Petersburg).

- Can't afford new materials like these? Make your own building sets by cutting out pictures of buildings from catalogs or magazines and pasting them onto empty boxes of various sizes. Children love to create their own cities or magical realms.

2. Allow children enough time to get deeply involved in the activities.

- Observe to see which activities draw the most attention and keep children occupied for the longest periods. Make a note of it. Allow children enough time to finish what they are doing even if this means they must postpone snack or story time. Children lose interest if the activities of their choice are interrupted before they finish. How would you feel?

- Keep an interesting activity going as long as you can. For instance, if children enjoy playing with water, make a list or keep a card file of all the water activities you can think of and bring out a new one when children finish the current ones. Have water table activities, such as filling plastic bottles using funnels and pitchers. Make suds with detergent and egg beaters. Make paper boats to sail in the water table. Take buckets of water and large paintbrushes outside to paint on sidewalks or walls.

- Eliminate turn-taking in activities that call for children to spend long periods when learning how something works. Computer learning games are a case in point. If you have been giving children 5-minute or even 10-minute turns on the computer, you will soon discourage them from using it because this is not enough time for them to become deeply involved in any of the games. Allow pairs of children to use the computer as long as necessary while they are teaching themselves how a game works. This helps expand their attention spans as well.

3. Integrate the most successful and longest-lasting activities into every learning center.

- Choose one of the books children want to hear again and again, for example, *Stella Luna,* and design a number of follow-up activities in various learning centers. Stella Luna is the baby fruit bat who falls off its mother's back into a bird's nest and has to live like a bird. Obtain the CD-ROM from Library Video Company (1-800-843-3620) and have pairs of children play the story games, clicking on objects in the jungle scenes. Have children make bat wings and bird wings in the art center. Reenact the story in the dramatic play center.

- Learn about night animals such as raccoons, opossums, cats, and owls in the science center. Build a zoo for plastic jungle animals in the block building center. Write a story about one of the night animals in the writing center. Record it on a tape cassette in the language center. Make up words and sing a song about Stella Luna in the music center.

Allow pairs of children to use the computer as long as necessary to learn a new game and to stretch their attention spans.

• When topics of great interest are integrated into the entire curriculum, the attention spans of many children are stretched accordingly to accommodate the activities they like most. When children are given choices among many activities that pique their interest and enough time to complete them, attention spans increase and behavior problems decrease. As Isenberg and Jalongo (1993) conclude:

> *Time conveys a clear message about the importance of an activity. When children have long blocks of time, their play is more constructive, cooperative, and expressive than with short, interrupted time periods. (p. 176)*

REFERENCES AND SUGGESTED READINGS

Barron, M. (1999). Three- and four-year-olds completing 150-piece puzzles? Impossible! *Young Children, 54*(5), 10–11.

Beaty, J. J. (1999). *Prosocial guidance for the preschool child.* Upper Saddle River, NJ: Merrill/Prentice Hall.

Eliot, L. (1999). *What's going on in there? How the brain and mind develop in the first five years of life.* New York: Bantam Books.

Isenberg, J. P., & Jalongo, M. R. (1993). *Creative expression and play in the early childhood curriculum.* Upper Saddle River, NJ: Merrill/Prentice Hall.

Nelsen, J., Erwin, C., & Duffy, R. (1998). *Positive discipline for preschoolers* (2nd ed.). New York: Three Rivers Press.

Sigman, M. (1997). "Why does infant attention predict adolescent intelligence?" *Infant Behavior and Development, 20,* 133–140.

Children's Book
Cannon, J. (1993). *Stella Luna.* San Diego: Harcourt.

3 ATTENTION-SEEKING

CONCEPT

Almost everyone wants to be noticed by someone. It is an important part of being human. Young children seek attention from their parents and caregivers, their siblings and friends, their teachers and classmates, as well as other people around them. If no one at home responds positively, or if a new baby has replaced them as the center of attention, they may try to call attention to themselves in school by tagging along with the teacher, always looking around to see if the teacher is noticing them, pushing ahead of others, interfering with others' activities, or being noisy and unruly. It is as if they are saying: "Look at me! I'm important, too! I can make you pay attention to me!"

Even if their disruptions result in scolding or punishment, they have achieved their goal: to make someone notice them, to get someone's attention. Although some children act out in the classroom because they have been treated harshly at home, others are really trying desperately to get the teacher to notice them, even with a negative response. How will you know which kind of acting-out is for attention and which is not?

One simple way is to watch the child who is causing the disruption. Does he or she continually look around to see if the teacher notices? Does the child persist with his interruptions no matter what the teacher says? He is one who in all probability is asking for your attention because he doesn't receive it at home. What should you do?

Some psychologists might tell you to ignore such disturbances unless they are serious, because to acknowledge them will only cause the child to do the same thing again whenever he wants attention. A better way is to go over to the child quietly—not shout at him across the classroom—pull him aside, and talk with him calmly about what he is doing. How does he feel? Is he upset or cross about something? What would make him fell better? Rather than imposing your will upon an upset child, ask him what would help. If you treat the child calmly without harsh words, you may be surprised how quickly he will respond in a reasonable manner. As Gartrell (2001) tells us:

> When a teacher removes a child from a situation and helps the child calm down so the two can then talk about, and hopefully resolve the conflict, the intervention is often positive, leading to important learning. (p. 8)

In the meantime there are positive actions you and your staff can take with the child on a one-to-one basis every day to make sure he realizes he is being noticed. This list of steps is long but you and your staff can plan to carry out some of the actions daily until the child realizes you really notice and care about him.

STEPS

1. **Speak kindly to the child.**
2. **Use nonverbal communication.**
3. **Listen to the child and respond.**
4. **Use the child's name and picture often.**
5. **Demonstrate your acceptance of the child.**

FIGURE 3–1   "Me and My
Favorite Colors: Orange, Red, and
Purple."

6. **Read and act out an attention-getting book.**
7. **Talk with the child's parents.**

ACTIVITIES

1. **Speak kindly to the child.**
   - Greet him every day when he comes in. For bilingual children say some words in their home language. Say "goodbye" daily and "I'll see you tomorrow." Point out something positive he has done. Offer encouragement and compliments. Tell him you have missed him after an absence.
2. **Use nonverbal communication.**
   - Smile and nod when you look at her. Touch her or give her a hug when appropriate. Give her high-fives. Get down to her level when speaking to her.
3. **Listen to the child and respond.**
   - Ask how he is feeling and listen to his answer. Ask for his opinion and respond to what he says. Follow his suggestions and ideas when appropriate.
4. **Use the child's name and picture often.**
   - Use the child's name when you talk with her. Put her name on her cubby and her products. Give her a name tag to use for turn-taking. Mention her name when talking with other children. Have the child paint a picture of herself and a favorite thing. (See Figure 3–1.) Take photos of the child and things she likes to do.
   - Sing songs using the child's name. Use some of the traditional nursery rhyme songs but make up your own words using children's names. For instance, *(Where Is Thumbkin?)* "Where is Jonathan? Where is Jonathan?" or *(Are You Sleeping?)* "Are you reading? Are you reading? Jen and Alison, Jen and Alison?"
   - Here are a few songs you may want to convert. (See Figure 3–2.) Be sure to use every child's name eventually and not just the children who need attention.

FIGURE 3–2 Nursery Songs for
Name Conversion.

Down by the Station

Go in and out the Windows

Here We Go Looby Loo

Here We Go Round the Mulberry Bush

Hickory Dickory Dock

I'm a Little Teapot

Jack and Jill

John Jacob Jingleheimer Schmidt

London Bridge Is Falling Down

Mary Had a Little Lamb

Row, Row, Row Your Boat

Shoo Fly

Three Blind Mice

Twinkle, Twinkle Little Star

Wheels on the Bus

5. **Demonstrate your acceptance of the child.**

  • Ask the child to help you do a chore. Choose the child for a special endeavor. Play a board
    game or make a puzzle with the child. Choose the child to be a leader. Give the child a
    chance to be first in some activities.

6. **Read and act out an attention-getting book.**

  • Read **Noisy Nora** (Wells, 1997) about the little mouse-girl who tries to get her parents'
    attention away from her brother and sister by banging the window and door, dropping her
    sister's marbles, knocking over the lamp, and other disruptions. Children love the comical
    illustrations and two-sentence rhymes on each page.

  • **No, David!** (Shannon, 1998). David's attention-getting problem occurs at home where he
    does everything he can to get his mother's attention, but all he hears is her voice saying, "No,
    David!" He walks across the living room with muddy feet, fills the bathtub to overflowing,
    runs down the street with no clothes on, bangs on a pan with a ladle, makes a potato man
    with his food, jumps on his bed with his cowboy boots on, and plays baseball in the living
    room until he breaks a vase. But finally his mother gives in, calls him over to her, and gives
    him a big hug, saying "Yes, David, I love you!"

  • **Peter's Chair** (Keats, 1967) is the classic story of a child who feels he is being replaced by a
    new baby. First his cradle and then his unused crib are being painted pink for his new sister.
    Oh, no, his little chair could be next. He decides to run away. Finally, his father involves him
    in helping to paint the chair.

  • Choose characters and reenact the story. Just reading a story to young children does not mean
    they truly understand what it is about. Stories that they really enjoy and want you to read
    again and again are ones they can come to understand by taking on the roles of the
    characters as you read the book again. They do not need to dress in costumes although some
    like to wear headbands or tags with a character's name. Talk with them about how they think
    the character should act and why, but then let them play the role any way they want. Repeat
    the reenactments as many times as you have children who want to be characters. Then leave
    the book and name tags in the dramatic play center for children to make up their own stories.

  • Use puppets. Another way to reenact stories is to use puppets or little plastic block people for
    the characters. You don't need a puppet stage but only the puppets themselves for children to
    act out their roles as you read the story.

The teacher can take the child aside, get down to his eye level, and talk calmly with him about his actions and what would make him feel better.

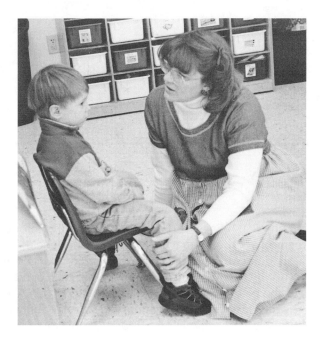

7. **Talk with the child's parents.**
   - Be sure to talk with the parents of children who seem to need special attention. Be positive, letting them know what you are doing to help their child get along in the class and feel good about himself. Do not point out the disruptive actions of the child, but how he is responding positively to the activities you are involving him in.
   - Give the parents a list of the songs, books, and activities their child likes. Show parents pictures their child has painted and photos of the child. Ask about how the child is getting along at home and what else you can do to help him at school.

REFERENCES AND SUGGESTED READINGS

Beaty, J. J. (1995). *Converting conflicts in preschool.* Clifton Park, NY: Thomson Delmar Learning.

Cherry, C. (1983). *Please don't sit on the kids: Alternatives to punitive discipline.* Belmont, CA: Fearon Pitman.

Fox, L., Dunlap, G., Hemmeter, M. L., Joseph, G. E., & Strain, P. S. (2003). The teaching pyramid: A model for supporting and preventing challenging behavior in young children. *Young Children, 58*(4), 48–52.

Gartrell, D. (2001). Replacing time-out: Part one—Using guidance to build an encouraging classroom. *Young Children, 56*(6), 8–16.

Hearron, P. F., & Hildebrand, V. (2005). *Guiding young children* (7th ed.). Upper Saddle River, NJ: Merrill/Prentice Hall.

Children's Books

Keats, E. J. (1967). *Peter's Chair.* New York: Scholastic.

Shannon, D. (1998). *No, David!* New York: Blue Sky Press (Scholastic).

Wells, R. (1997). *Noisy Nora.* New York: Dial/Penguin.

BEHAVIOR, INAPPROPRIATE

CONCEPT

Young children are physical beings who express their feelings through their behavior. If they are feeling good about themselves, their behavior is generally positive. If things are not going well for them or they are feeling bad about themselves and their circumstances, they often express this condition through disruptive, unruly behavior. They may throw, hit, kick, or bite; they may run around wildly and shout or scream. In the past, early childhood practitioners often referred to such actions as *negative* behavior. Because words and their connotations are so powerful, we prefer to use a different term today. We call such troublesome actions *inappropriate* behavior.

Too often in the past when we spoke of a child's "negative" or "bad" behavior, we began to think of the child as negative or bad. This is not the case. It is the behavior that is negative, not the child. On the other hand, if you think of unruly behavior as *inappropriate* (which it is), you are more likely to respond with supportive actions that can help the child learn to use appropriate behavior. Negative behavior seems to call for punishment or punitive discipline, while inappropriate behavior calls for guidance.

This text discusses both the appropriate and inappropriate behavior of young children. (See inside front cover.) Thirteen types of inappropriate behavior are dealt with. As a teacher of young children you may think that an important part of your role is to curb this behavior by stopping it, lessening it, changing it, redirecting it, converting it, or eliminating it. That is not the case.

Actually, it is the child behavers themselves who are the most important role players in this learning situation. It is these children who must learn how they can stop, lessen, change, redirect, convert, or eliminate their own inappropriate behavior. And it is you, the teacher, who will help them learn how through the guidance procedures described in this text.

Where does a child's behavior come from? Behavior is determined by a child's social-emotional makeup. Eliot (1999) describes how this social-emotional growth evolves from a child's genetics and environment.

> Each child is born with his or her own unique emotional makeup, what we often refer to as "temperament." But this innate bent is then acted upon by the unique environment in which the child is reared—by his history of tenderness or abuse, cuddling or criticism, attention or neglect, discipline or disorder, and by the forms of emotional display and social interaction he sees modeled by those around him. (p. 291)

You realize that what we call *appropriate behavior* is helpful behavior, while what we call *inappropriate behavior* is often harmful behavior. As a teacher of young children you can affect this behavior by your own emotional display and social interaction that you model daily in the classroom. In addition you can help a child understand and change his own inappropriate behavior once you understand it yourself.

STEPS

1. **Observe to find out all you can about the child's inappropriate behavior.**
2. **Make a positive change in one of the actions you observed to see if it affects the behavior.**
3. **Focus on how children who disrupt feel and what would make them feel better.**

ACTIVITES

1. **Observe to find out all you can about the child's inappropriate behavior.**
   * Figure 4–1 lists questions you need to answer about the child's inappropriate behavior. Using the observation techniques discussed in Chaper 1: Assessing Behavior, you may find, for instance, that a) the child goes around interrupting activities other children are involved in by knocking down block structures, messing up art, taking doll clothing and throwing it; b) this behavior occurs mainly in the morning when the child enters the classroom; c) the children being interrupted are usually individuals playing by themselves; d) the behavior stops when the "victim" either hits him, cries, or runs to the teacher; e) the child "aggressor" stands nearby and looks at the teacher as if waiting for his punishment; and f) the teacher scolds the child or sends him to a time-out chair.

2. **Make a positive change in one of the actions you observed to see if it affects the behavior.**
   * In this instance, when the staff found through observation that the child's disruptive behavior occurred mainly when he entered the classroom in the morning, they decided to change the way they interacted with him from the start. They felt the child was trying to get the teacher's attention in this inappropriate manner. They decided they needed to do more than give him a perfunctory "Hi" or "Good to see you," and nothing else.
   * The teacher and staff made an extra effort to greet the child very warmly when he came in and to get him involved in an activity of his choice right away. If he couldn't seem to choose anything, the teacher invited him to play a game or make a puzzle with him, or to choose a book the teacher would read to him. Once the child got involved, his inappropriate behavior mostly stopped. All of the staff members kept an eye on this child to make sure he was involved in activities.

3. **Focus on how children who disrupt feel and what would make them feel better.**
   * In addition, the teacher stopped punishing the child for disrupting another child's activity, but instead took him aside and talked about feelings. He encouraged the child to come to him

FIGURE 4–1 Questions to be Answered About a Child's Inappropriate Behavior.

What does it consist of?

When does the child do it?

How often?

What other children or adults are affected by it?

How is it stopped or redirected?

What happens then?

Teachers can often help a disruptive child by participating in an interesting activity with him.

when the child was feeling out-of-sorts. He would help him watch what the others were doing, talk about it, and get him involved in something he was interested in. It worked. This teacher definitely agreed with Gartrell's (2002) findings:

> *When adults teach children to solve social* [and emotional] *problems, rather than punish them for having problems they have not yet learned to solve, they are using guidance. (p. 36)*

REFERENCES AND SUGGESTED READINGS

Dunn, M. (2003). Getting along while getting ahead: Meeting children's social and emotional needs in a climate of academic accountability. *Dimensions of Early Childhood, 31*(3), 18–26.

Eliot, L. (1999). *What's going on in there? How the brain and mind develop in the first five years of life.* New York: Bantam.

Gartrell, D. (2002). Replacing time-out; Part two—Using guidance to maintain an encouraging classroom. *Young Children, 57*(2), 36–43.

Marion, M. (2003). *Guidance of the young child* (6th ed.). Upper Saddle River, NJ: Merrill/Prentice Hall.

www.challengingbehavior.org The Center for Evidence-Based Practice: Young Children with Challenging Behavior.

www.pbis.org The Technical Assistance Center on Positive Behavioral Interventions and Supports (PBIS).

5 COMMUNICATING FEELINGS

CONCEPT

One of the most difficult things for young children to deal with is their feelings. When someone hurts them, they may cry. When someone takes their toys, they may hit or push. When someone tries to make them do something they don't want to do, they may whine, run away, or sit on the floor and pout. Young children tend to express their feelings very directly with actions. What they tend not to do is express their feelings in words.

What are some of their difficult feelings? Fear (or anxiety) is one. It is often caused by the presence of something threatening or the absence of safety or security. Fright-producing elements can include strange people and places, barking dogs, snakes, loud noises, thunderstorms, lightning, or the dark. Taking young children to a new place or leaving them with a babysitter are fear-producing for many children. They may hide, run away, cling to someone, or cry. Sadness is also a difficult feeling for young children. When someone goes away, when a person or a pet is ill or dies, when they have to move, or when something unpleasant happens in their families, children often feel sad or distressed. They may mope around, refuse to eat, or cry.

Anger and frustration are other difficult feelings for most children. When someone takes something from them, forces them to do something or stop doing something, when someone pushes or hits them or calls them a name, they may get red in the face, cry, or run to the teacher. Some just hang their heads and move away. But others may resort to aggressive retaliation such as hitting, biting, kicking, spitting, or throwing things. What they rarely resort to is expressing their feeling in words. Why is that?

Most young children do not understand what they are feeling. The words "angry," "afraid," "worried," "upset," "sad," or "unhappy" have little or no meaning for them. Then why do children express their feelings in the actions described? As Nelsen et al. (1998) tells us:

> Children learn to cope with their feelings by watching their parents. And all too often, parents deal with difficult feelings either through emotional displays (dumping their stronger emotions on the people around them) or by squelching them entirely. (pp. 17–18)

But when they are in a classroom full of children like themselves, all the youngsters need to learn a more appropriate way of expressing their unpleasant feelings rather than acting out. They need to learn to communicate what they are feeling in words. Words are powerful diffusers of feeling. If children can say in words what they are feeling inside, some of the bottled-up energy of the emotion is released. Using words rather than actions to express how they feel makes them feel much better right away. It also helps those around them relate to what they are saying and to understand how they feel. It is up to you, a teacher or volunteer, to help children learn the words that describe their feelings.

STEPS

1. **Be a model.**
2. **Be a coach.**
3. **Identify and name the emotions.**

4. Read a book about emotions.

5. Do art, creative movement, and dramatic activities.

ACTIVITIES

1. Be a model.

- Be a model yourself using words to express how you feel during an emotional experience. For example: "Oooh! That siren really startled me! But it's okay now. How do you feel?"

- Share your emotional experiences with individual children. For example, when a child runs over to you because a large dog is on the playground, you can shoo away the dog and comfort the child, but also say, "When I was little, big dogs used to frighten me, too. How do you feel?"

2. Be a coach.

- Be a coach for children experiencing a strong emotion. Tell them what to say. For example: "Tell him how you feel, DeWayne. Don't hit him!" or "Tell her what happened to her doll, Jessica. Don't just push her away!" If you talk like this to individuals enough times, soon they will be repeating you. You will hear them tell other children: "Tell him in words, Tyrell. Don't hit him!"

3. Identify and name the emotions.

- Identify and name the emotions you see the children experiencing by the looks on their faces and their gestures.

- Have posters showing emotions. Put them up one at a time and discuss each one. Help children learn to identify and name them. Lakeshore (1-800-421-5354) offers a pack of 20 posters showing children's moods and emotions. Figure 5–1 lists several emotional words children should learn to identify.

4. Read a book about emotions.

- Read a book, such as those listed in Figure 5–2, about children experiencing some of the difficult emotions such as fear, anger, worry, sadness, or jealousy. Afterward have a discussion about how the book characters handled the situation, especially the words they used.

- Read *That Makes Me Mad!* Every two pages in this book shows Nina trying to solve a problem that makes her mad: trying to get dressed without success, being blamed for spilling water when it was her little brother's fault, hearing her mom talk about her to others as if she's not even there, having her parents break a promise they made to her, when it's her turn and nobody will listen, and when she knows where she put something and it isn't there. In the end Nina's mother let's Nina tell her how angry she is, and that makes Nina feel better. Read the book to two children at a time and ask them what Nina should say after each problem-solving try.

- Read one of the books in Figure 5–3, which includes *The Little Old Lady Who Was Not Afraid of Anything* (Williams, 1986). Children enjoy this folktale-like story about the little old lady who was walking through the woods at night when strange things started following her: a pair of shoes going clomp, clomp; a pair of pants going wiggle, wiggle; a shirt going shake, shake; white gloves and a black hat going clap, clap, and nod, nod; and a big orange jack-o-lantern going boo, boo. But they couldn't scare her, she told them. That made them sad until she

FIGURE 5–1 Emotional Words Expressing Difficult Feelings.

Fear:	afraid	Anger:	angry	Sadness:	sad
	scared		mad		unhappy
	fearful		cross		depressed

This teacher asks children to identify how they are feeling from this poster of children's faces, and to tell why they feel as they do.

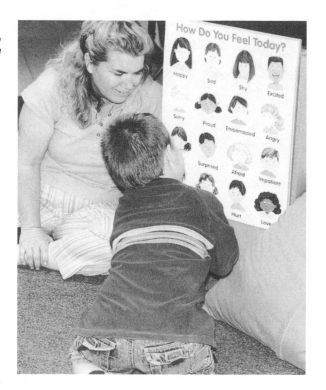

FIGURE 5–2 Books About Anger.

> *Mean Soup* (Everitt, 1992)
>
> *Sometimes I'm Bombaloo* (Vail, 2002)
>
> *That Makes Me Mad!* (Kroll, 2002)
>
> *When Sophie Gets Angry—Really, Really Angry* (Bang, 1999)

FIGURE 5–3 Books About Fears.

> *Chicken Chickens* (Gorbachev, 2001)
>
> *The Little Old Lady Who Was Not Afraid of Anything* (Williams, 1986)
>
> *Francis the Scaredy Cat* (Boxall, 2002)
>
> *Green Snake Ceremony* (Watkins, 1997)
>
> *The Owl Who Was Afraid of the Dark* (Tomlinson, 2001)
>
> *Storm is Coming!* (Tekavec, 2002)

whispered to the pumpkin head what to do, and they did it: they made a scarecrow in the garden to scare away the crows.

- Have a story reenactment. Bring in shoes, pants, shirt, gloves, hat, and a paper jack-o-lantern for the children to use for a story reenactment. Have children choose which item to be and have them trail around the room trying to scare the old woman as you read the story. The old woman must use words to express her feelings. Then have them make up their own version.

5. **Do art, creative movement, and dramatic activities.**
   - Do art, creative movement, and dramatic activities about stories the children have listened to, giving them a chance to experience the characters' emotions vicariously and thus learn what to say themselves. After discussing one of the emotional words (example: sadness), see if children can draw pictures, like the one shown in Figure 5–4, of themselves experiencing this emotion.

FIGURE 5–4 This Child Said She Felt Sad Because She Dropped Her Food. Perhaps She Doesn't Understand What Smiley Faces Show.

REFERENCES AND SUGGESTED READINGS

Beaty, J. J. (1995). *Converting conflicts in preschool.* Clifton Park, NY: Thomson Delmar Learning.

Beaty, J. J. (1999). *Prosocial guidance for the preschool child.* Upper Saddle River, NJ: Merrill/Prentice Hall.

Nelsen, J., Erwin, C., & Duffy, R. (1998). *Positive discipline for preschoolers.* New York: Three Rivers Press.

Vance, E., & Weaver, P. J. (2003). Words to describe feelings. *Young Children, 58*(4), 45. From: *Class meetings: Young children solving problems together.* Washington, DC: National Association for the Education of Young Children.

Children's Books

Bang, M. (1999). *When Sophie gets angry—Really, really angry.* New York: Blue Sky Press.

Boxall, E. (2002). *Francis the scaredy cat.* Cambridge, MA: Candlewick.

Everitt, B. (1992). *Mean soup.* San Diego, CA: Harcourt Brace.

Gorbachev, V. (2001). *Chicken chickens.* New York: North South Books.

Kroll, S. (2002). *That makes me mad!* New York: SeaStar Books.

Tekavec, H. (2002). *Storm is coming.* New York: Dial Books.

Tomlinson, J. (2001). *The owl who was afraid of the dark.* Cambridge, MA: Candlewick.

Vail, R. (2002). *Sometimes I'm Bombaloo.* New York: Scholastic Press.

Watkins, S. (1997). *Green snake ceremony.* Tulsa, OK: Council Oak Books.*

Williams, L. (1986). *The little old lady who was not afraid of anything.* New York: HarperCollins.

*multicultural

6 CONFLICT CONVERSION

CONCEPT

Within the hustle and bustle of a lively early childhood classroom, children can't help but encounter one another sometimes by accident, sometimes in a friendly exchange, but sometimes in a more serious and even aggressive manner. When two come together, each wanting his or her own way, or own toy, or own turn, more often than not it becomes a conflict. Most of these conflicts are resolved by the children themselves as they go on about their business. But some interpersonal encounters seem to resist an easy settlement and may eventually call for a different resolution.

Should you intervene? If the children in your classroom are constantly running to you to settle their squabbles, it may be because they are used to adults controlling their lives. This text, on the other hand, describes strategies in which the children themselves learn to resolve many of their conflicts. When children assume responsibility for their own behavior, their conflicts tend to lessen and their solutions tend to be longer-lasting. We need to give children every opportunity to work out their own solutions. There are times, however, when the teacher or staff member must intervene. Such times include:

- When there is crying
- When there is hitting or throwing things
- When one child hurts another
- When one child is being victimized
- When a child is damaging materials
- When the conflict escalates beyond the children's bounds
- When the conflict reaches an impasse

If children are unable to settle their own disagreements, or if actions become violent or emotions get out-of-control, it is time for an adult to step in. Before you do, however, you need to consider carefully what you are involved with: *Conflicts are not bad, and the children who cause them are not bad.* Instead, every early childhood conflict is a learning opportunity. You should be thankful for this opportunity to be able to teach children at this young age how to handle difficult situations. Crosser (1992) points out:

> Conflict is a natural part of living and working together in groups. It is good that conflicts arise in the early childhood classroom because it is only through facing conflicts that children can learn the skills necessary to resolve real-life problems. (p. 28)

This text defines conflict as "interpersonal encounters needing positive emotional resolutions." Children who learn to convert conflicts to positive feelings in early childhood carry with them the powerful tools to convert adulthood conflicts, as well. Many of the conflicts young children encounter in the classroom will be similar to ones they may meet later in life in much more serious circumstances. They include:

- Attention-getting conflicts
- Blaming or fault-finding conflicts
- Group entry disputes

- Name-calling
- Out-of-control superhero play
- Personality conflicts (jealousy)
- Possession disputes
- Power struggles

Each of these conflicts is discussed under a separate strategy in this text. The discussion here describes a general strategy for converting any kind of conflict to positive feelings.

If you as a teacher, student teacher, or staff member in an early childhood classroom find that you must intervene in a clash between two children, how will you do it? In earlier times teachers simply waded in and stopped the clash, then punished the child who started it. These days such an approach is seldom effective or appropriate. On the contrary, incidents of aggression have continued and violence has increased according to many early childhood teachers (Carlsson-Paige & Levin, 1992). One Head Start teacher reports:

> Aggression has increased and has become the primary first choice in a child's attempt to settle a dispute or resolve a conflict. For example, a child will lash out and hit immediately if someone threatens him, rather than using a less aggressive response. (Worstell, 1993)

How should you intervene in such a situation? There is a new method that this author and a colleague have developed that almost always stops the conflict and prevents it from recurring. We call it "other-esteem conflict conversion." There is no blame or shame involved for, after all, these children have not yet learned how to handle conflict. Here is how it works:

STEPS

1. **Calm yourself and the children involved before proceeding.**
2. **Ask each child to tell you what has been happening.**
3. **Ask each child to tell you how she thinks *the other child* feels.**
4. **Ask each child to tell you what will make the other child feel better.**

ACTIVITIES

1. **Calm yourself and the children involved before proceeding.**
   - No matter how loud or violent the conflict has been, you must remain calm and in control. You can take the two conflictees aside to a quiet place in the classroom where you can talk with them if necessary. Take them by the arms and speak softly as you move them away from the scene of the conflict. Hum a little tune or whisper their names if you think that will help. Wait for them to calm down before proceeding.
2. **Ask each child to tell you what has been happening.**
   - Get down to the child's eye level and ask them one at a time what has been happening. Start with either one, for you understand there is no blame or shame involved. Listen carefully without comment to what each child says. Thank each for telling you. Their stories will undoubtedly be different because each is coming from her own point of view. She may be trying to blame the other and expects *her* to be punished.
   - For example, Samantha says Kayla took her character doll when she put it down for a minute and wouldn't give it back. It's all her fault. On the other hand, Kayla says Samantha hit her and grabbed the doll away from her. It's her fault. You should thank them both for telling you what has been happening, but say that we're not talking about whose fault it is. We just want to find out what happened. Now we know that Kayla took Samantha's doll and Samantha hit her and grabbed it back.

3. **Ask each child to tell you how she thinks *the other child* feels.**

   - What a surprising question for most children! The answer to this question starts the other-esteem conflict conversion. When you ask Samantha how she thinks Kayla feels, there is often a long pause. Perhaps she is wondering why Kayla should feel anything when it's her fault. She took the doll. Ask Samantha again to think about how Kayla feels. Ask her to look at Kayla's face. Finally she says that Kayla looks angry. Yes, Kayla agrees. She is angry because Samantha hit her.

   - Now ask Kayla the same question: How does she think Samantha feels? Kayla, too, is surprised by the question. She would rather talk about why it is Samantha's fault and not hers. Tell her yes, you said that before, but now we're talking about feelings. How does she think Samantha feels? Finally Kayla says that Samantha looks angry. Samantha agrees.

   - These feeling questions about the other person are a surprising turn of events for most children. They are used to having an adult try to find out whose fault it is, and then to punish that child. Instead, you are asking them to think about how the other child feels. This shifts the conflict away from them and asks them to consider the other child's feelings. Most children can tell how another person feels and will answer accurately when they see you are not blaming them.

4. **Ask each child to tell you what will make the other child feel better.**

   - Ask Samantha what she thinks will make Kayla feel better. By now Samantha realizes you are truly interested in feelings and not whose fault it was. Samantha also understands that Kayla wants her doll, but should she have to give it up? Not unless she wants to. It should be her decision. She may decide to share the doll with Kayla if Kayla agrees. She does.

   - Then ask Kayla what she thinks will make Samantha feel better. Well, maybe they could find another character doll and play together with both dolls. Samantha quickly agrees, and off they go. Children's resolutions like this are often more creative and appropriate than any you could have devised; plus they give the children ownership of the outcome, thus diffusing future possible conflicts over dolls.

   - Be sure to thank the children for working out the problem of who should play with the dolls. Do they know of any better way to get one of the dolls when someone else is playing with it besides hitting and grabbing? Yes, they both decide that they could ask the other person.

Ask each child to tell you how the other child feels. This is the "conflict conversion" question.

Children often think of wonderfully creative and appropriate resolutions to a conflict.

For some children learning to ask permission is a huge step up the ladder of peaceful social interaction. If it can be learned without blaming or shaming anyone, it is a lesson that may last a lifetime. As Adams and Wittmer (2001) reiterate: "Early childhood teachers report an increase over the last 5 to 10 years in the number of children coming to school angry, aggressive, or lacking the social skills to get along with classmates" (p. 10).

Whenever you have to intervene in a conflict between two children, consider using this other-esteem conflict conversion technique. We have found that it works much better than teacher-controlled resolutions. It may take a few minutes longer, but they are minutes worth investing when the children themselves decide on an appropriate resolution.

REFERENCES AND SUGGESTED READINGS

Adams, S. K., & Wittmer, D. S. (2001). "I had it first." Teaching young children to solve problems peacefully. *Childhood Education, 78*(1), 10–14.

Beaty, J. J. (1995). *Converting conflicts in preschool.* Clifton Park, NY: Thomson Delmar Learning.

Beaty, J. J. (1999). *Prosocial guidance for the preschool child.* Upper Saddle River, NJ: Merrill/Prentice Hall.

Carlsson-Paige, N., & Levin, D. (1992). When push comes to shove—Reconsidering children's conflicts. *Child Care Information Exchange, 84,* 34–37.

Crosser, S. (1992). Managing the early childhood classroom. *Young Children, 47*(2), 23–29.

Kemple. K. M. (2004). *Let's be friends: Peer competence and social inclusion in early childhood programs.* New York: Teachers College Press.

Wheeler, E. J. (2004). *Conflict resolution in early childhood: Helping children understand and resolve conflicts.* Upper Saddle River, NJ: Merrill/Prentice Hall.

Worstell, G. (1993). Unpublished interview. Human Development Corporation Head Start, Columbia, MO.

7 CONFLICTS, GROUP ENTRY

CONCEPT

Teachers of young children whose classrooms are set up in a learning-center style recognize that group entry conflicts are one of the most frequent types to occur. Some children are always wandering around from group to group, trying to become involved with what the other children in the different learning centers are doing. More likely than not, those children will not permit a newcomer to join in the activities they are already engaged in.

What is the outsider to do? He or she may try to force his way in, argue with the children involved, take one of their materials, throw a tantrum, or run to the teacher. You, on the other hand, may tell the child to go play with his own materials or you may even force the group to allow the outsider to play. Neither of these solutions is particularly helpful, and more problems with this child may occur later.

But why should they occur in the first place, you may wonder? Can't young children choose to play in one group or go to another without all this trouble? Ramsey (1991) has this to say about it:

> Interactions in preschool classrooms are short, so children are constantly having to gain entry into new groups. The process is made more difficult because children who are already engaged with each other tend to protect their interactive space and reject newcomers. (p. 27)

Child development researchers have studied this problem over the years, observing strategies various young children use to gain entry into group play. They conclude that certain strategies almost always work, whereas others usually fail. By putting their findings to use you can help unsuccessful children gain access to group play without resorting to physical or verbal assaults.

These researchers conclude that many children need more than one strategy to gain access, and that such strategies should be tried in a certain order (Corsaro, 1979; Dodge, Schlundt, Schocken, & Delugach, 1983; Ramsey, 1991; Shantz, 1987). The strategies are:

1. **Child should watch and listen to the group**
2. **Child should then play parallel to the group**
3. **Child should then make a play-oriented statement to the group**

You can help unsuccessful children gain entry to such play groups in the following manner:

STEPS

1. **Observe and record behaviors of children who try to enter ongoing play but are unsuccessful.**
2. **Coach children who need help entering groups.**
3. **Use conflict conversion strategies with children who disrupt play.**
4. **Help everyone become involved in activities they like at the start of the free-choice period.**

A child trying to enter a group should make a play-oriented statement to the group.

ACTIVITIES

1. Observe and record behaviors of children who try to enter ongoing play but are unsuccessful.

- Just as you did with assessing behaviors, you can observe children who are unsuccessful in gaining access to ongoing group play. Some teachers take notes in the form of a running record, writing down what happens when a child tries to enter a group. Other teachers prefer to use a checklist like the one in Figure 7–1, which points out behaviors they may otherwise overlook.

2. Coach children who need help entering groups.

- While it is true that most children learn social skills such as group entry by making attempts on their own, some children need your help: not your intervention with the group, but your coaching help in which you suggest what they should do. You can tell Alex to stand nearby and watch what Tyler and Dion are doing. When Alex notes that they are playing with push-button equipment, you can suggest that Alex find a toy cell phone and play with it near the group. When the time is right he can make a group-oriented statement such as: "My cell phone works like yours. See?" Most play groups allow outsiders to contribute to and join their play if approached indirectly like this.

3. Use conflict conversion strategies with children who disrupt play.

- Alex disrupted the play of Tyler and Dion by taking a piece of their equipment and running off with it, causing Dion to chase and hit him. You will need to: a) take both boys aside and ask each what is happening; b) ask each boy how he thinks the other boy feels; and finally, c) ask each boy what he thinks would make the other feel better. If the conflict has really been converted, they should be able to find a solution that both can agree upon so the problem will be settled.

4. Help everyone become involved in activities they like at the start of the free-choice period.

- If you anticipate group entry problems with certain children, you can try to avoid them by helping children become involved in activities at the start of the free-choice period. Your classroom should already be set up with a number of interesting learning centers, but you can put out special activities you know will attract certain children.
- Ask who would like to use the cartoon character stampers to make their own comic strips. You can choose two or three children, including the ones who have trouble getting involved. Other interested children can sign up (name scribbles are okay) on a sign-up sheet and take

FIGURE 7–1 Group Entry
Strategies Checklist.

Name _____ **Observer** _____

_____ Watches what playgroup is doing

_____ Plays near group with similar materials

_____ Makes group-oriented statement ("I know how to do that.")

_____ Enters group successfully

_____ Asks "Can I play?"

_____ Is rejected but tries again

_____ Makes aggressive claim ("That's mine!" or "I was here first!")

_____ Disrupts play physically

_____ Is rejected and does not try again

_____ Complains to teacher

Note: The publisher grants permission to reproduce this checklist for evaluation and record keeping.

Most play groups allow outsiders to contribute to their play if approached indirectly.

their turns when the first ones are finished. Do the same with the other activities. When children are occupied in activities of their choice, they seldom become involved in group-entry conflicts.

• Read and discuss a book about children having access troubles (see Figure 7–2) to one small group at a time that includes children who have this problem.

FIGURE 7–2   Books With Access
Problems.

> Alexander, M. (1981). *Marty McGee's Space Lab, No Girls Allowed.*
> Graham, B. (1996). *This Is Our House.**
> Havill, J. (1989). *Jamaica Tag-along.**
> Kurtz, J. (1990). *I'm Calling Molly.**

*multicultural

REFERENCES AND SUGGESTED READINGS

Beaty, J. J. (1995). *Converting conflicts in preschool.* Clifton Park, NY: Thomson Delmar Learning.

Beaty, J. J. (1999). *Prosocial guidance for the preschool child.* Upper Saddle River, NJ: Merrill/Prentice Hall.

Corsaro. W. A. (1979). "We're friends, right?" Children's use of access rituals in a nursery school. *Language in Society, 8,* 315–336.

Dodge, K. A., Schlundt, D. C., Schocken, I., & Delugach, J. D. (1983). Social competence and children's sociometric status: The role of peer play group entry strategies. *Merrill-Palmer Quarterly, 29*(3), 309–336.

Ramsey, P. G. (1991). *Making friends in school: Promoting peer relationships in early childhood.* New York: Teachers College Press.

Shantz, C. U. (1987). Conflicts between children. *Child Development, 58,* 283–505.

Singer, E., & Hannekainen, M. (2001). The teacher's role in territorial conflicts of 2- and 3-year-old children. *Journal of Research in Childhood Education, 17,* 5–18.

Wheeler, E. J. (2004). *Conflict resolution in early childhood.* Upper Saddle River, NJ: Merrill/Prentice Hall.

Children's Books

Alexander, M. (1981). *Marty McGee's space lab, no girls allowed.* New York: Dial Books.

Graham, B. (1996). *This is our house.* Cambridge, MA: Candlewick Press.

Havill, J. (1989). *Jamaica Tag-along.* Boston: Houghton Mifflin.*

Kurtz, J. (1990). *I'm calling Molly.* Morton Grove, IL: Whitman.*

———

*multicultural

CONFLICTS, POSSESSION

CONCEPT

When young children enter your classroom full of its wonderful toys and marvelous materials—all for them, it can be quite overwhelming at first. Many children do not understand that the toys and materials are not for them alone, but must be shared with other children. Being at an egocentric stage of their development, they often try to take any toy they want even when another child has possession. Thus, many of the first and most numerous conflicts you and they will encounter are possession disputes. Child development researchers also agree with Hay (1984), who reports:

> It is evident that one common source of conflict in early childhood, as in adult society, is the struggle for the possession of tangible resources; in children's groups, these usually consist of toys and other play materials. (p. 14)

Hay found that possession disputes comprise 90% to 100% of the conflicts in some programs. One child tries to take the toy or material away from another child who will not give it up, resulting in a conflict. Happily most of these conflicts are brief, lasting only a few minutes or even a few seconds. Most are settled by the children themselves, often by one child giving up the toy or the other child going on to something else. It is only when one child forcibly takes another's toy, causing crying or hitting, that teachers need to intervene.

You may wonder why such conflicts occur in the first place, when the classroom is so full of toy trucks, blocks, dolls, puppets, books, puzzles, science tools, dress-up clothes, manipulatives, music makers,

When one child tries to take a toy away from another who won't give it up, conflict often results.

crayons, and paint. The materials themselves are not the main problem. It is young children's egocentric nature that keeps them focused on their own point of view and limits their understanding of what another child wants. As they begin to develop "other esteem," i.e., how another child feels, they will learn to share and take turns with toys. Learning to deal with possession disputes helps teach them this. That is why it is essential that the children, not you, resolve their conflicts.

Observe the children in your classroom to determine who is involved in possession disputes. As the school year progresses, these conflicts seem to decrease in frequency as children find ways to resolve them on their own. You may find, like the researchers did, that it is the same few children who continue to be involved repeatedly. They may need your help in learning necessary interpersonal skills.

In the meantime, set up the learning centers in your classroom to provide enough materials for several children to use at one time; introduce new materials ahead of time; and set up a turn-taking arrangement for using them (see Chapter 48: Turn-taking).

STEPS

1. **Help children learn what to say to avoid possession conflicts.**
2. **Stock centers where conflicts usually occur with an abundance of materials.**
3. **Provide more than one of a favorite toy.**
4. **Introduce new materials ahead of time and set up a turn-taking arrangement.**

ACTIVITIES

1. **Help children learn what to say to avoid possession conflicts.**

   - When you see two girls struggling over a cell phone that both want, and know from previous experience this will undoubtedly lead to an explosive conflict, you should intervene before it happens. Take one of the girls aside and ask *whether she has asked the other* to use the phone. The answer is usually "no," she didn't ask because she knew the other girl would never give it up. Suggest that she try asking anyway. "Maybe if you ask in a nice way, she will give you a turn with the phone." *Coaching a child* on what to say is often enough to resolve the problem. If it isn't, you can suggest that she "make a deal" with the girl. Can she think of something she can trade for a chance with the phone? For instance, she might decide to trade her turn at the computer for the phone. How can she say that? Have her practice on you. With a little coaching on what to say, children can often come up with an acceptable compromise.

   - Read a book with characters involved in a possession conflict to a small group. Read *This Is Our House* (Rosen, 1996), about a group of city children playing outside with a cardboard box they have turned into a house. George is in the house and will not let any of the other children inside. No matter what they say, he pushes them away. Ask your listeners what they would say to persuade George to let them in.

   - Use puppets to help children learn what to say in possession disputes. Use two puppets with a child who frequently fights over toys. Put one on your hand and give the other to the child. Tell him your puppet has a toy truck he wants, and his puppet needs to find a way to get the truck without a fight. Does he use words to ask your puppet? If not, suggest that he try. Then switch roles and have his puppet be the one with the toy and your puppet trying to get it by using words. Have this brief puppet play on a daily basis to help children learn to use words in their possession confrontations.

2. **Stock centers where conflicts usually occur with an abundance of materials.**

   - *Block Building Center.* Ramsey (1986) found that 78% of the classroom materials involved in children's possession disputes were blocks.

     Some specific functions of the blocks that were most often associated with conflict were the use of blocks to create boundaries, the accumulation of blocks in individual building projects, and the creation of structures with small openings such as garages. (p. 177)

- You can help diffuse this problem by stocking the block center with enough unit blocks for several children to build large buildings. Instead of purchasing a set or kit, it is better to order large numbers of units, doubles, and quadruples, the most useful and popular kinds of blocks, along with smaller numbers of columns, ramps, and arches.

- *Manipulative/Math Center.* Ramsey also found that manipulatives were the most frequent objects of conflict when two or more children were trying to use the same objects or to accumulate objects. Give children many materials to play with. Fill your shelves with plastic see-through boxes of:

Buttons	Shells	Sorting blocks
Chips	Dice	Pegs
Stacking blocks	Dominoes	Golf tees
Nesting cubes	Slotted wheels	Play money
Snap blocks	Animal counters	Shape beads
LEGO blocks	Stringing beads	Plastic gears
Bristle blocks	Pattern blocks	Nuts and bolts

- Also include many puzzles of different sizes, game boards, pegboards, sectioned boxes, egg cartons, several toy cash registers, carpenter's rules, and scales.

3. **Provide more than one of a favorite toy.**

- Have you noticed which toys the children seem to clash over? Try to have more than one of these toys available. For instance, have several egg beaters and basters in the water table, several trikes on the playground, several toy binoculars or telescopes, several toy cell phones, several cash registers, and several firefighter's hats. These are favorite materials in many classrooms.

4. **Introduce new materials ahead of time and set up a turn-taking arrangement.**

- Introduce the new material when all the children are together, perhaps at a morning circle. Talk about how to use it and pass it around for children to try it. Then put it on a shelf with a

When learning centers have enough materials, children play peacefully.

name label. Ask the children how they would like to take turns using it. Depending on the material, they may suggest a sign-up sheet or a kitchen timer. Rules children make for themselves are more likely to be followed. When other possession conflicts arise they may remember to use the same rules.

REFERENCES AND SUGGESTED READINGS

Adams, S. K., & Wittmer, D. S. (2001). "I had it first." Teaching young children to solve problems peacefully. *Childhood Education, 78*(1), 10–16.

Beaty, J. J. (1995). *Converting conflicts in preschool.* Clifton Park, NY: Thomson Delmar Learning.

Beaty, J. J. (1999). *Prosocial guidance for the preschool child.* Upper Saddle River, NJ: Merrill/Prentice Hall.

Hay, D. F. (1984). Social conflict in early childhood. *Annals of Child Development, 1,* 1–44.

Kemple, K. M. (2004). *Let's be friends: Peer competence and social inclusion in early childhood programs.* New York: Teachers College Press.

Ramsey, P. G. (1986). Possession disputes in preschool classrooms. *Child Study Journal, 16*(3), 173–181.

Children's Book

Rosen, M. (1996). *This is our house.* Cambridge, MA: Candlewick Press.

9

CRISIS, CHILDREN IN

CONCEPT

One of the difficult child behavior situations teachers find themselves facing today concerns children who suffer from a family crisis such as a breakdown of the family or child abuse. Family breakdowns may be caused by divorce, hospitalization, incarceration, job loss, or the death of a family member. A more personal crisis for too many children is abuse: emotional abuse, physical abuse, or sexual abuse by someone in the family or close to it. This may result in the child being placed outside the home with relatives or in a foster home. Any of these scenarios can cause severe emotional upheaval in young children whether or not they display it immediately.

Thus, it is essential that the teacher keep in touch with a child's family, especially when emotional problems surface with the child. When a cheerful, easy-going child suddenly turns morose or withdrawn, or reverts to baby talk or wetting, the child may not want to or be able to explain why she feels this way. Talking with parents when they drop off or pick up their youngsters is one possible time to find out if anything has changed at home. Often parents are not aware of how deeply their children are affected by what goes on at home. Has someone lost a job? Does someone need to be hospitalized? Is someone getting a divorce? Does someone plan on leaving?

Parents themselves should be discussing such situations with their children, reassuring them that they will be taken care of, that they will be all right. But often parents do not, perhaps because it is so emotional for them as well. In some instances children, with their egocentric point of view, may think that they are the cause of the situation—especially in the case of a divorce.

With child abuse there are other more stringent rules you must follow in reporting, investigating, and follow-up. Be sure to learn what they are from the center director or school principal. But in all of these crisis situations you must first look to the child involved to see how you can help him or her deal with the dilemma.

STEPS

1. **Stay physically close to the child.**
2. **Focus complete attention on the child.**
3. **Allow the child to continue expressing feelings.**
4. **Help the child to talk when ready.**

ACTIVITIES

1. **Stay physically close to the child.**

   - Children who are suffering from an emotional disturbance need to know that you are near and will support and comfort them in any way possible. Farish (2001) tells us:

     Physically holding children brings comfort and a sense of security. At times like these, young children need extra hugs, smiles, and hand-holding. Reassure them that they are safe and that there is always someone there to take care of them. Hearing a family member or teacher say: "I will take care of you," helps a child feel safe. Young children have great faith in adults' powers and respond to adult reassurances. (p. 6)

- Even if children do not allow you to touch or hold them, stay as close as they will allow. You can be talking in a soft, low voice that can comfort them. Perhaps if you put out a hand near their own hand, they will take hold of it or allow you to place it on their shoulder.

2. Focus complete attention on the child.

- The teacher or one of the classroom staff members should focus her complete and undivided attention with no interruptions on a child suffering from emotional pain. She can play with him on a one-to-one basis in whatever he chooses to do. Set aside a space inside the classroom for this "special time" kind of play (Bowling & Rogers, 2001, p. 80). Have available all kinds of puppets, clay, beanbags with faces on them and targets to throw at, or pillows to throw or kick or hit. (See chapter 24: Materials, calming.) The teacher can follow the child's lead in the activity, allowing the child to succeed or to win a game.

3. Allow the child to continue expressing feelings.

- Do not try to stop the child from crying, wailing, whining, screaming, or however else she is expressing the emotional hurt she feels. She needs to be able to vent her feelings, to release the emotions pent up inside her in order to heal. Remember, crying is not the hurt but the healing. If children are not allowed to vent feelings, those feelings may emerge later as kicking or hitting. Or the children may push them inside and retreat to a corner to suck a thumb, and it could take hours or days rather than minutes to become themselves again. Children need to move through difficult and painful emotions in their own way for this to happen. Teachers can help by letting children know that it's okay to be angry; it's okay to be afraid; it's okay to cry (Bowling & Rogers, 2001, p. 81).

4. Help the child to talk when ready.

- Verbalizing strong emotions helps children to diffuse them. You can help them to express what they are feeling—but only if they are ready. Talking about things to a supportive adult helps children gain a sense of control. But, as Farish (2001) reminds us:

  Children should not be pressured to talk. They may need time to absorb the experiences before discussing them, or they may have other ways of communicating. (p. 6)

Focus complete attention on the child and play with him on a one-to-one basis in whatever he chooses to do.

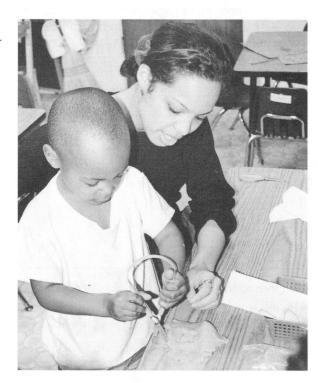

- You may need to sit silently nearby as long as necessary, giving the child time to think about what has happened. Then you may want to start talking yourself, hoping the child may join in. If not, there are other methods for encouraging children to talk.

- Depending on the situation, you may want to read an appropriate book to the child. Sometimes a book about a child facing an upsetting situation may help the child to talk about her own problems. For girls a book such as *Sometimes I'm Bombaloo* (Vail, 2002) tells an outrageously illustrated story of what Katie does when she loses her temper. It's scary for Katie and those around her when she becomes Bombaloo. But when her unruly actions cause something funny to happen and she laughs, then she's Katie again. What would your child do?

- For boys a book to read is *Mean Soup* (Everitt, 1992), about Horace who has such a bad day he hisses and growls when he gets home instead of talking to his mother. She puts on a top hat, her dance costume, and begins making mean soup in a pot of water on the stove. She throws in some salt and then starts screaming into the pot. Now it's Horace's turn and he screams, growls, and bares his teeth. He sticks out his tongue twenty times and breathes his best dragon breath. When he can finally smile, they know the soup is done and together they stir away the bad day.

- You could make mean soup with your child, too, if it seems appropriate. Will this help him to talk? Books like this are so valuable you should plan to order them from your library if you do not own a copy.

REFERENCES AND SUGGESTED READINGS

Bowling, H. J., & Rogers, S. (2001). The value of healing in education. *Young Children, 56*(2), 79–81.

Dozier, J. (2004). Four ways to help children in crisis. *Dimensions of Early Childhood, 32*(2), 14–18.

Farish, M. (2001). Helping young children in frightening times. *Young Children, 56*(6), 6–7.

Hyson, M. (2004). *The emotional development of young children: Building an emotion-centered curriculum* (2nd ed.). New York: Teachers College Press.

Koplow, L. (Ed.) (1996). *Unsmiling faces: How preschools can heal.* New York: Teachers College Press.

Solter, A. (1992). Understanding tears and tantrums. *Young Children, 47*(4), 64–67.

Children's Books
Everitt, B. (1992). *Mean soup.* San Diego: Harcourt Brace.

Vail, R. (2002). *Sometimes I'm Bombaloo.* New York: Scholastic Press.

10 EMERGENCIES

CONCEPT

Emergencies in early childhood programs present an entirely different guidance situation for the classroom staff. In this often unstable world of ours, unexpected events seem to happen on a regular basis. Catastrophic occurrences that affect everyone include natural disasters from floods, hurricanes, tornados, or earthquakes (see chapter 41: Storms), as well as man-made emergencies from fires, accidents, crashes, shootings, or explosions.

Whether or not these happenings affect young children depends upon how close they are to the events, whether they or someone they know is directly involved, and how they see you respond. As a member of a classroom team you may be dealing with children exhibiting fear and panic when disaster strikes. What should you do?

Before an emergency occurs you must consider carefully how you would respond. You cannot afford to panic when the children are dependent upon you and the other adult staff members. What about fear? It is human to feel fear about fires, explosions, and shootings. Can you find ways to contain this fear while you protect and comfort the children? As Farish (2001) explains:

> Helping young children deal with their feelings and thoughts is especially challenging when we adults haven't had time to deal with our own reactions, when we are grieving, afraid, and angry. We should remember that even very young children notice a great deal and they can quickly tune into any sorrow or anxiety that surrounds them. (p. 6)

STEPS

1. **Before an emergency you should control your fears and help children to control theirs.**
2. **During an emergency you should respond in ways you have practiced with the children.**
3. **After an emergency you should help children become engaged in activities that will calm them.**

ACTIVITIES

1. **Before an emergency you should control your fears and help children to control theirs.**

   - Think it over. What will it take to calm yourself when you hear sirens blaring or the building fire alarm ringing? The following steps are suggestions some teachers use both for themselves and the children. Talk it over with the staff and then try them. Introduce them to the children and practice them. Whenever you hear a siren outside, have the children stop what they are doing and practice these emergency steps:

     1. Close eyes and take several deep breaths
     2. Count to 10 or 20
     3. Hum or sing softly
     4. Say, "Help is on the way"

FIGURE 10–1 Books About Fire
Fighters and Emergency Vehicles.

> *A Day in the Life of a Firefighter* (Hayward, 2001) *
>
> *Emergency!* (Mayo, 2002)*
>
> *Even Firefighters Hug their Moms* (MacLean, 2002)
>
> *Fire Fighters* (Simon, 1995)
>
> *Fire Fighters A to Z* (Demarest, 2003)*
>
> *Fireman Small* (Yee, 1994)
>
> *Mighty Machines: Fire Trucks and Other Emergency Machines* (Bingham, 1995)
>
> *New York's Bravest* (Osborne, 2002)*
>
> *Stop Drop and Roll* (Cuyler, 2001)

*multicultural

- You are a model for the children. When children see that the teacher or staff member is not upset, it helps to calm them down as well. In addition children enjoy following steps with the teacher leading them. You can say: "Now everybody close your eyes. Take 3 deep breaths. One, two, three. Now everybody hum, *Row, Row, Row Your Boat.*" Can the children hum? They will have fun learning how. Make some humming noises for them to copy. Finally, say: "Now everybody say together: *Help is on the way.*" Do they feel better yet? Try it again.

- Read the picture book *Emergency!* (Mayo, 2002) to the children. This is an important book for the classroom to own these days. It shows a different emergency vehicle on every other page (police car, ambulance, lifeboat, fire engine, etc.) going to the rescue with lights flashing and sirens blaring. At the end of each brief text are the lines: "Help is coming. It's on the way." Use the books in Figure 10–1 to help children speculate about such emergencies: what caused them and what happens when the emergency vehicles get to the scene.

- Children can pretend about emergencies after hearing this book or others by playing "emergency" in the block center with Stack & Roll Emergency Vehicles, wooden community vehicles, block play people, or the complete fire station with vehicles and firefighters from Lakeshore Learning Materials (1-800-778-4456).

- After hearing a story about an emergency it is important for children to reenact the story with dress-up hats and costumes (Lakeshore) to help them understand and clarify their ideas about sirens, emergency vehicles, and help. Becoming personally involved like this also helps to diffuse fears they may have—especially if they understand: "help is on the way." Another fine book actually showing a little boy and his sister dressing up and playing firefighter, police officer, emergency medical technician, helicopter pilot, and other roles is *Even Firefighters Hug their Moms* (MacLean, 2002).

2. **During an emergency you should respond in ways you have practiced with the children.**

- Emergency evacuation of the building should be one of the situations you have prepared the children for in case of fire, earthquake, or chemical emergencies. Drills can be held ahead of time with children learning to follow particular rules. Practice the procedure shown in Figure 10–2 repeatedly so that everyone understands how to do it without panic. Use a real fire alarm or smoke alarm to acclimatize children to the ear-splitting noise. Emergency exiting demands rules and order: no straggling or out-of-control behavior. Practice exiting calmly again and again until children get it right. Have one of the children use a stopwatch to keep track.

- An emergency duffel bag should be prepared ahead of time and kept in a special location near the door. Contents of the bag are shown in Figure 10–3. The center director or school principal will designate a primary and secondary evacuation site. You can practice evacuating to each of the sites. Children enjoy the challenge of these drills even when an

FIGURE 10–2 Rules for
Emergency Exiting of a Building.

- Line up children quickly but calmly.
- Teacher at head of line; staff members at rear.
- Teacher carries emergency duffel bag and daily attendance sheet.
- Follow quickest safe route to outside.
- Assemble at evacuation site outside building.
- Count to make sure all children are present.

Note: From *Safety in preschool programs* (p. 88) by J. J. Beaty, 2004. Upper Saddle River, NJ: Merrill/Prentice Hall.

FIGURE 10–3 Contents of
Emergency Duffel Bag.

- Bottled water
- Paper cups
- Snacks (crackers, dried fruit)
- Battery-operated radio and extra batteries
- Blanket
- First aid supplies and handbook
- Emergency contact information for each child and staff member
- Cell phone
- Cards describing games and songs

Note: From *Safety in preschool programs* (p. 80) by J. J. Beaty, 2004. Upper Saddle River, NJ: Merrill/Prentice Hall.

alarm is sounding. You will have prepared them ahead of time for the noise and they will learn to endure it. When they see that you are calm, they will be, too.

- Children can help you choose ahead of time what to put in the duffel bag. They can choose the snacks, as well as the games and songs you will be playing at the evacuation site. When you get there during practice runs, stay long enough to play a game, sing a song, and eat a snack. As you can tell, this makes emergency exiting exciting and interesting, not frightening.

3. **After an emergency you should help children become engaged in activities that will calm them.**

- Children need to wind down from an emergency. They may all want to talk at once about what happened. One way to encourage talking yet keep things in control is to bring out community workers hand puppets (perhaps six) and ask children to choose one to wear. Have all the children sit in a circle and listen to what each puppet has to say. To get things started ask a child's puppet: "Who are you?" or "What did you do?" Listen, comment, and question. Then go on to the next puppet. When all six puppets have spoken, ask children who have not had a turn to choose one of the puppets and speak if they still have things to say.

- If you do not have proper puppets, children can make their own from small paper bags with the bottom turned flat for a face. Put out colored peel-off stickers for eyes, nose, and mouth, or use felt-tip markers. Children can name their puppets and speak for them if they choose to.

- Cooking or making play dough is another calming activity. Children in small groups can stir away their emotions as they take turns stirring flour and water to make dough (see also chapter 24: Materials, calming).

- Getting back to normal is important after an emergency. Children need to feel that the routines they are used to are still in operation. Teachers can talk to the children about what will happen for the rest of the day, following the regular schedule as much as possible. If

Children need to reenact emergency scenarios from books by dressing up in emergency hats or costumes.

Children can choose to play with puppets that portray community workers.

children did not eat the snack at the evacuation site, now would be the time. What routines are they used to? What about hand washing before eating and listening to a story before the food is passed out? These normal routines can help children feel that things are getting back to normal. As Alat (2002) concludes:

> *Providing structured, stable, and predictable routines, consistent rules, and immediate feedback will help children to feel more secure after a traumatic event. (p. 5)*

REFERENCES AND SUGGESTED READINGS

Alat, K. (2002). Traumatic events and children: How early childhood educators can help. *Childhood Education. 79*(1), 2–7.

Beaty, J. J. (2004). *Safety in preschool programs.* Upper Saddle River, NJ: Merrill/Prentice Hall.

Farish, M. (2001). Helping young children in frightening times. *Young Children, 56*(6), 6–7.

Greenman, J. (2002). *What happened to the world? Helping children cope in turbulent times.* New York: Bright Horizons Family Solutions.

Marin Child Care Council (2000). *Childhood emergencies: What to do.* Boulder, CO: Bull Publishing Co.

Uhlenberg, J. M. (1996). After the alarm rings. *Young Children, 51*(2), 46–47.

Children's Books

Bingham, C. (1995). *Mighty machines: Fire trucks and other emergency vehicles.* Boston: Houghton Mifflin.

Cuyler, M. (2001). *Stop drop and roll.* New York: Simon & Schuster.

Demarest, C. L. (2003). *Fire fighters A to Z.* New York: Aladdin Paperbacks.*

Hayward, L. (2001). *A day in the life of a firefighter.* New York: DK Publishing.*

MacLean, C. K. (2002). *Even firefighters hug their moms.* New York: Dutton's Children's Books.

Mayo, M. (2002). *Emergency!* Minneapolis, MN: Carolrhoda Books.*

Osborne, M. P. (2002). *New York's bravest.* New York: Alfred A. Knopf.*

Simon, N. (1995). *Fire fighters.* New York: Simon & Schuster.

Yee, W. H. (1994). *Fireman Small.* Boston: Houghton Mifflin.

---

*multicultural

11 EMOTION MODELING

CONCEPT

Most young children look to the adults around them when upsetting things happen or dangerous situations arise. They are not only seeking adult direction on what to do, but also how adults are responding emotionally to the situation. They look at adults' faces to see if they are smiling, frowning, or not reacting emotionally at all. They listen to the tone of adults' voices to hear if they are friendly, angry, or fearful. As Hyson (2004) reports:

> *Starting as early as 12 months, children are especially likely to look to adults for emotional information in new, uncertain situations, a process that has been called "social referencing."* (p. 67)

Such behavior on the part of infants and young children makes sense when you realize they have not yet learned how to act in new situations. It is from observing other people that they gain ideas to guide their own actions. Even infants can remember and copy the complex behaviors they see (Hyson, p. 66). Researchers have also found that children who frequently see adults showing empathy, generosity, and frustration tolerance are more likely to develop these qualities themselves (Eisenberg & Fabes, 1998).

What does this mean for you and your staff? If adults' unintentional emotional expression has such an impact on young children's behavior, then early childhood teachers should take advantage of this important emotion-modeling process and use it to help children learn how to manage their own behavior.

STEPS

1. **Choose several emotional responses you would like children to recognize.**
2. **Look for appropriate situations and model the specific emotions.**
3. **Observe and record how children respond to such situations over time.**

ACTIVITIES

1. **Choose several emotional responses you would like children to recognize.**
   - As you consider your classroom situation and your own emotional temperament, think of several important happenings that call for an emotional response from you. Be sure your focus is positive and the emotion you express is an appropriate, positive, and genuine one. For example:

     Pleasure: for a child sharing or helping another; for a child expressing anger in words, not actions

     Pride: for a child whose behavior has improved; for a child completing a difficult task

     Caring: for someone who is sick; for someone who needs comforting

     Anger managing: for someone who has hurt another; for someone who has damaged materials

2. Look for appropriate situations and model the specific emotions.

- How do you express pleasure when you see a child sharing or helping another? Some teachers smile, clap their hands, and say: "Good for you, Vanessa. You let Nicole borrow your best doll. Here, let me shake your hand." To express pleasure when Kyle says to an angry Anthony: "Tell Carlos in words, Anthony! Don't hit him!" . . . you may pat Kyle on the back, smile, and say: "Thanks, Kyle, for telling Anthony to say why he's angry in words."

- How do you express pride over something difficult a child has done? Some teachers are more animated than others in their expression of emotions. Do you clap your hands? Clasp your hands together and shake them vigorously? Shake the child's hand? Give the child a "high five"? Say, "Hooray! You finally did it!" Have a huge smile on your face? Hold the child's hand up like he's a winner? The more animated and expressive you can be, the more that child and others will like it. Try to use the very same expression every time you see a child accomplishing a difficult task. That way they understand how much their success meant to you, and they themselves may try to do the same thing another time.

- Modeling caring emotions may be the easiest of all. When someone falls and scrapes a knee, you hurry to her side to help her up, comfort her, clean and bandage the scrape, and later ask how she feels. When someone has been absent because of illness, you welcome him back, ask how he feels, and tell how much you missed him.

- What about anger? How do you manage anger when you are upset about something a child has done? You do not have to shout or use an angry tone of voice. You can talk in even tones without being harsh, and show by your facial expression how you feel. You should definitely express your feelings in words: "I'm very upset by what you've done, Kyle—pushing the tape recorder off the table like that. If it's broken, then no one can use it!" Then you might add in a softer tone: "Let's pick it up and see."

- Be spontaneous and genuine about modeling emotions when the occasion occurs, but also plan some modeling scenarios when you know the children are watching.

- Children can learn to model these emotions, not only by imitating you, but also by practicing with puppets or little block people. You and the child can reenact various scenarios. In each case you can ask the child how one of the characters should respond in order to show pleasure, pride, caring, or anger management.

- Another time read a book that requires characters to show an emotion toward something another has done. In *Please, Baby, Please* (Lee & Lee, 2002), baby is a little toddler who pours cereal on her head, makes crayon marks on the wall, tries to eat sandbox sand, and pursues other activities only a toddler can think up. Her caregivers treat her gently, saying "please, baby, please," rather than scolding or punishing her. At night after she has been put to bed, she toddles into her mother's bedroom saying: "Kiss me goodnight? Mama, mama, mama, please."

3. Observe and record how children respond to such situations over time.

- If you and the staff are working on remembering to show *pleasure* when individuals do something nice, *pride* when someone has accomplished something difficult, *caring* when someone needs comforting, and *anger management* when you are upset by a child, be alert to see if any children are imitating you. Hyson (2004) notes:

  As a teacher and classroom leader, you have more power than you may think. Children model themselves on those who hold the key to the resources they desire—not candy and stickers, but your attention and sincere approval. (p. 74)

- A teacher can increase a child's chances of imitation by helping him focus on the behavior she models. She can actually call attention to a nearby child to watch what she is about to do. For example, when DeWayne keeps jumping up and down on the blocks, she can call Mario over to watch how she handles it. As you see children beginning to imitate the teacher's emotions, make note of it and put it in each child's portfolio or other ongoing records.

This teacher calls one boy to watch how she is going to handle the situation of a second boy jumping up and down on the blocks.

- Emotion modeling by adults has a real effect on children. Research shows that positive emotions are contagious. Happier mothers had happier children. Parents who showed negative emotions, especially anger, had children who showed more negative emotions in independent situations (Denham, 1998). Thus, emotion modeling by teachers in early childhood classrooms can set the stage for emotion management in children.

REFERENCES AND SUGGESTED READINGS

Brazelton, T. B., & Sparrow, J. D. (2001). *Touchpoints 3 to 6: Your child's emotional and behavioral development.* Cambridge, MA: Perseus Publishing.

Denham, S. A. (1998). *Emotional development in young children.* New York: The Guilford Press.

Eisenberg, N., & Fabes, R. A. (1998). Prosocial development. In N. Eisenberg (Ed.), *Handbook of child psychology: Vol. 3. Social, emotional, and personality development* (5th ed.). New York: Wiley.

Hyson, M. (2004). *The emotional development of young children: Building an emotion-centered curriculum* (2nd ed.). New York: Teachers College Press.

Children's Book

Lee, S., & Lee, T. L. (2002). *Please, baby, please.* New York: Simon & Schuster.*

———————

*multicultural

12

ENVIRONMENT, CLASSROOM

CONCEPT

The physical environment of an early childhood classroom can add immeasurably to the positive behavior of children if it is set up to be child-centered. It should include learning centers set up with young children's independent activities in mind. What are learning centers? They are specific activity areas set up by the teacher with help from the children to encourage independent learning on the part of the child. Children will be able to choose which centers to work in, what materials to use, and how to use the materials. In most early childhood programs, learning centers include: blocks, books, dramatic play, science/discovery, manipulatives/math, art, music, writing, computer, sand/water, and woodworking. Large motor activities are also featured within some classrooms, especially if there is a loft. Sloane (2000) has this to say about them.

> Centers in early childhood classrooms provide ideal environments for active learning. Open-ended in nature, they support activities that challenge children as well as expose them to concepts appropriate for their ages and abilities. Centers set the stage for meaningful hands-on exploration, experimentation, and practice. (p. 16)

STEPS

1. **Clearly arrange enough learning centers to keep children comfortably engaged.**
2. **Make centers easily accessible to all children with materials on low shelves facing out.**
3. **Have enough materials for several children at once; change when interests change.**
4. **Have several inviting private spaces within the classroom. (See Figure 12–1.)**

ACTIVITIES

1. **Clearly arrange enough learning centers to keep children comfortably engaged.**
   - For children to be independent and self-directed in their learning, they need to be able to see what is available. Your learning centers can be delineated by dividers made from low shelves pulled out from the wall, from filmy material strung from rods or clotheslines, or from furniture such as couches.
   - The size of the classroom and number of children help to determine the size and number of the centers. For classes of 18 to 20 children consider having three large centers to accommodate 4 to 6 children at once (blocks, dramatic play, and books), five medium centers for 4 children (science, manipulatives, art, writing, and sand/water), and two small centers for 2 children (computer and woodworking). Ratcliff (2001) notes:

     > Research shows that placing young children in relatively small areas may increase aggressive behavior. More accidental physical encounters occur in crowded areas. Young children don't see a difference between accidental and intentional actions and respond with aggression. (p. 84)

FIGURE 12–1 Child-Centered
Learning Centers Checklist.

Learning Centers General Conditions

_____ Centers clearly delineated with low dividers or shelves

_____ Located to avoid large empty spaces

_____ Enough centers to keep children comfortably engaged

_____ Room enough for several children at once

_____ Light and sunny, sound-proofed

Accessibility

_____ Space enough to enter and leave center easily

_____ Accessible to children in wheelchairs, walkers, braces

_____ Materials on low shelves, facing out

_____ Room traffic patterns wide enough for free movement

_____ Traffic patterns short and winding enough to prevent running

Materials

_____ Enough for several children at once

_____ More than one of favorite toy

_____ Outlets for expressing feelings

_____ Colored to create emotional tone

_____ Changed as interests change

Private Spaces

_____ Cubbies, shelves, boxes for private possessions

_____ Mattress or floor pillows in quiet corner

_____ Overstuffed chair or couch

_____ Old bathtub or inflated pool with pillows

_____ Large carton with door cut out

_____ Card table covered with blanket

2. **Make centers easily accessible to all children with materials on low shelves facing out.**

   - Children should be able to come and go easily as their interests shift. Thus centers should not be completely closed in. Small entrances can cause pushing and shoving or attempts to keep newcomers from entering. As Ramsey (1991) has noted:

     Interactions in preschool classrooms are short, so children are constantly having to gain entry into new groups. This process is made more difficult because children who are already engaged with each other tend to protect their interactive space and reject newcomers. (p. 27)

   - Blocks, books, toys, and materials on the low shelves should face out, not sideways, so children can easily see what is available. Keep it simple. Crowding shelves with too many items makes it difficult for children to make choices, and thus may spark squabbles.

3. **Have enough materials for several children at once; change when interests change.**

   - Observe to see which materials are the most popular and have several of each on hand. Be sure to have four pairs of safety goggles at the water table and two at woodworking. Children love eggbeaters and basters in the water table, trucks in the block center, and firefighters' hats in the dramatic play center. You can prevent many squabbles by having more than one or two.

   - Make the centers colorful. Use fabrics, flowers, and colorful vinyl coverings. Bead curtains add interest as well as color. A colored light bulb in a lamp can make a dramatic play area exciting or mysterious. Paper lanterns, balloons, and green glass fishnet floats have other

Small entrances can cause shoving or attempts to keep newcomers from entering.

effects. Taylor (2002) tells us: "Because color can be the single most powerful visual cue in attracting the attention of young children, it should be chosen with special care." She recommends red for gross motor areas; yellow for music and art; and green, blue, and purple for reading areas (p. 369).

- Change the materials from time to time: different books in the book center, new arrangements in the dramatic play center (a store or clinic instead of housekeeping), new pictures and posters on the walls, new materials to explore in the science center (sink-and-float water experiments instead of magnets or magnifying glasses). Variety should be the spice of life in children's centers, too. Have children help make the changes.

4. Have several inviting private spaces within the classroom.

- Many children need a break from the sometimes overstimulating classroom environment. Some teachers provide an overstuffed chair in a quiet corner. Others put floor pillows in a playhouse or pup tent. An old bathtub or an inflated pool filled with pillows are other possibilities. The space on top of or under a small loft can serve the same purpose. Whatever private spaces you create, be sure they are within the classroom and not isolated outside. Children need to experience some private time but they also like to see what others are doing. Bunnett and Davis (1997) tell us:

    We discovered that children need more than one "cozy nest," and designed several soft and quiet places. We found that with additional quiet spaces children can do their work with fewer disruptions, feel less fatigued, and can retreat to a quiet place without negative connotations. (p. 44)

REFERENCES AND SUGGESTED READINGS

Bunnett, R., & Davis, N. L. (1997). Getting to the heart of the matter. *Child Care Information Exchange, 114*, 42–44.

Clayton, M. K. (2001). *Classroom spaces that work: Strategies for teachers series.* Greenfield, MA: Northeast Foundation for Children.

Fye, M. A. S, & Mumpower, J. P. (2001). Lost in space: Design learning areas for today. *Dimensions of Early Childhood, 29*(2), 16–22.

Kemple, K. M. (2004). *Let's be friends: Peer competence and social inclusion in early childhood programs.* New York: Teachers College Press.

Ramsey, P. G. (1991). *Making friends in school: Promoting peer relationships in early childhood.* New York: Teachers College Press.

Ratcliff, N. (2001). Use the environment to prevent discipline problems and support learning. *Young Children, 56*(5), 84–88.

Rushton, S. P. (2001). Applying brain research to create developmentally appropriate learning environments. *Young Children, 56*(5), 76–82.

Sloane, M. W. (2000). Make the most of learning centers. *Dimensions of early childhood, 28*(1), 16–20.

Taylor, B. J. (2002). *Early childhood program management.* Upper Saddle River, NJ: Merrill/Prentice Hall.

13 FAMILY INVOLVEMENT

CONCEPT

You can include family members in their child's classroom learning if you involve everyone at home and school together in promoting a simple but essential behavior children need to acquire: CARING. Caring is helping another, nurturing another, sharing with another, giving to another, comforting another, empathizing with another. It is important that children learn to care while they are young in order to counteract the amount of anger, rage, and violence that is reaching them through war scenes on television, neighborhood quarrels, and family aggression. Swick and Freeman (2004) worry that:

Without caring intervention, children's brains will be physically altered, not only by the violence they personally experience but also by the violence they observe. (p. 2)

They describe how constant exposure to violence and stress causes the release of cortisol in the brain, which can change brain activity and eventually alter the structure of the brain. For children it then becomes increasingly difficult to accurately interpret and respond to social situations. When young children see and experience people hurting one another as a common occurrence, they may come to accept it as normal behavior: that there is nothing wrong with it.

To neutralize these negative effects young children need a strong dose of caring: learning what caring is by being cared for themselves and learning how to practice it on others. The place to start is in the home. As Swick and Freeman (2004) tell us: "The most powerful message that children receive about caring is how they are cared for themselves during the earliest years of life" (p. 2).

How can you get families involved in emphasizing caring in their homes? One effective method is to create a "caring community" in the classroom that you ask families to support both at home and in school. "Caring" can be year-long theme in all the activities you do together. "We care for each other" can be your motto. You, the children, and their families can proceed in some of the following ways:

STEPS

1. **Create a chart of caring actions that children do for each other.**
2. **Have children look for caring actions performed by others and paste stickers on the chart when they see an action.**
3. **Send home a copy of the chart to the families, asking them to paste stickers on it when they witness caring.**
4. **Read books with caring themes to the children, asking them to tell what each character does to show caring; do story reenactments; send books home for families to read to their children.**
5. **Invite family members into the classroom to read these books to the children and do caring activities with them.**
6. **Have a family get-together like a potluck to celebrate caring.**

This may seem like a long list of steps, but it can be carried out—not all at once—but throughout the year along with other activities you, the children, and their families create such as caring songs, caring dances, caring games, or caring puppets.

46

FIGURE 13–1   How We Care for
Each Other.

By being a friend _____

By doing something nice for someone _____

By comforting someone _____

By feeling the way someone else feels _____

By giving something to someone _____

By helping someone _____

By letting someone take your turn _____

By saying kind words to someone _____

By sharing something with someone _____

By showing someone how to do something _____

ACTIVITIES

1. **Create a chart of caring actions that children do for each other.**
   - Talk to children about caring: that it is helping one another, sharing, giving, and caring for others. Then have them offer suggestions of what they can do to show they care for someone else. Write their suggestions on a chart with space to paste on stickers when someone sees an action being done. Have room on your chart to add new sharing items. (See Figure 13–1.)

2. **Have children look for caring actions performed by others and paste stickers on the chart when they see an action.**
   - In addition to having a large caring chart on the wall, you can print individual copies for each child's journal. When a child recognizes that someone is doing a caring action, that child gets to paste a sticker on the big chart and one on the small chart in the person's journal. For example, Meghan sees Sarah helping Xena with her learning center necklace. She tells the group and then gets to paste a sticker on the wall chart after "By helping someone," and also to paste a sticker on the chart in Xena's journal. Be sure to thank Sarah for being a helper and Meghan for recognizing it.

Caring can be helping a child tie her learning center necklace.

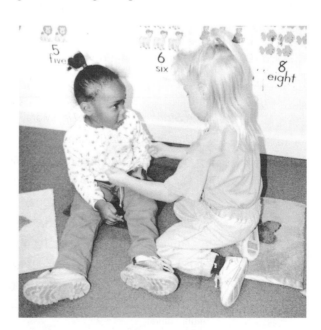

- If no one notices a caring action during the day, you can talk to the group at the end of the day and ask if anyone remembers seeing someone do a caring action. The caring actions need to be spontaneous ones, of course, and not something you or the children ask someone to do. See how long it takes for caring to take hold in your classroom. Children enjoy challenges like this, and some will not only keep their eyes peeled for caring, but will look for opportunities to practice caring themselves. Eventually caring actions will become second nature to everyone, and recognition and stickers will no longer be necessary.

3. **Send home a copy of the chart to the families, asking them to paste stickers on it when they witness caring.**

   - If you have parent volunteers in the classroom, they may have already contributed to making the chart. Otherwise, send a note home with the children that the class is becoming a "caring community" and that you hope the family will help at home by watching out for caring and putting stickers on the chart you are sending along with a baggie of stickers. Invite them to participate in the caring community by visiting the classroom to see what the children are doing, and bringing their own ideas, songs, and suggestions.

   - One parent wrote new words to a song the children liked to sing ("Where Is Thumbkin?"):

        We are caring, we are sharing,

        Watch us care, watch us share;

        Come and see our classroom,

        Come and see our classroom,

        Come and care, come and share.

   The teacher sent copies of the words to the other families and asked them to sing along and to contribute their own caring ideas. See Figure 3.2 in chapter 3 for a list of familiar songs that can be converted to "caring songs."

4. **Read books with caring themes to the children, asking them to tell what each character does to show caring; do story reenactments; send books home for families to read to their children.**

   - Figure 13–2 gives a selection of mostly multicultural books with caring themes. After reading each book, ask the children how the characters showed caring.

   - *Love Can Build a Bridge* shows wonderfully clear illustrations of children caring for one another in different situations on every two pages: being hungry, getting hurt, being in the hospital, falling down on rollerblades, fixing a bike tire, being scared of fireworks, wanting to read, and needing a bandage. A tape cassette of the Judds' song *Love Can Build a Bridge* comes with the book for everyone to sing. "Love can build a bridge. Don't you think it's time?" say the words. Is "love" caring? What do your children think?

FIGURE 13–2 Books With Caring Themes.

> *A Birthday Basket for Tia* (Mora, 1992)*
>
> *Dragonfly's Tale* (Rodanas, 1991)*
>
> *Four Friends Together* (Heap, 2003)
>
> *Full, Full, Full of Love* (Cooke, 2003)*
>
> *Homemade Love* (Hooks, 2002)*
>
> *I Love My Mama* (Kavanagh, 2002)
>
> *Jamaica Tag-Along* (Havill, 1989)*
>
> *Love Can Build a Bridge* (Judd, 1990)*
>
> *That's What Friends Do* (Cave, 2004)

*multicultural

Children can do spontaneous caring actions by helping to clean up without being told.

5. **Invite family members into the classroom to read these books to the children and do caring activities with them.**

   • If families have read the books at home, they will be familiar with them and should be more at ease reading in the classroom. Children enjoy hearing stories read over and over. Their meaning becomes more clear. Children can once again reenact the stories, this time with their families playing roles or making up their own stories.

6. **Have a family get-together like a potluck to celebrate caring.**

   • Be sure to recognize what everyone has contributed. Perhaps families can tell what has happened at home since they joined the class "caring community." Do children do spontaneous caring actions at the get-together?

REFERENCES AND SUGGESTED READINGS

Diffily, D. (2001). Family meetings: Teachers and families build relationships. *Dimensions of Early Childhood, 29*(3), 5–10.

Eisenberg, N. (1992). *The caring child.* Cambridge, MA: Harvard University Press.

Goldstein, L. (1998). More than gentle smiles and warm hugs: Applying the ethic of care to early childhood education. *Journal of Research in Childhood Education, 12*(2), 244–261.

Swick, K. (1997). A family-school approach for nurturing caring in young children. *Early Childhood Education Journal, 25*(2), 151–154.

Swick, K. J., & Freeman, N. K. (2004). Nurturing peaceful children to create a caring world: The role of families and communities. *Childhood Education, 81*(1), 2–8.

Warner, L., & Barrera, J. (2004). A nine-point guide to improving school/parent relationships. *Dimensions of Early Childhood, 32*(2), 3–7.

Children's Books

Cave, K. (2004). *That's what friends do.* New York: Hyperion Books.

Cooke, T. (2003). *Full, full, full of love.* Cambridge, MA: Candlewick Press.*

Havill, J. (1989). *Jamaica tag-along.* Boston: Houghton Mifflin.*

Heap, S. (2003). *Four friends together.* Cambridge, MA: Candlewick Press.

Hooks, B. (2002). *Homemade love.* New York: Hyperion.*

Judd, N. (1990). *Love can build a bridge.* New York: HarperCollins.*

Kavanagh, P. (2002). *I love my mama.* New York: Simon & Schuster.

Mora, P. (1992). *A birthday basket for Tia.* New York: Simon & Schuster.*

Rodanas, K. (1991). *Dragonfly's tale.* New York: Clarion Books.*

———

*multicultural

14   FAULT-FINDING

CONCEPT

"I didn't do it! It's his fault! He did it!" is a common refrain that sounds frequently in early childhood classrooms. Young children certainly know all about fault-finding. From early on they have heard adults around them looking for a culprit to blame when things go wrong. Because blame usually signals some kind of punishment, most children try their best to put the blame on someone else—anyone but themselves. Blame also makes children feel guilty because they may be ashamed of what they did. It is a distinctly low-down feeling.

These early moral emotions of shame and guilt seem to be the same throughout the world. Many early childhood researchers such as Jerome Kagan (1984) believe that emotions like these underlie the development of morality everywhere. The fear of punishment, social disapproval, or failure, as well as guilt over their own "shameful" behavior, are supposed to motivate children's development of morality.

Could there be a more affirmative way to help children develop the positive side of morality—i.e., the prosocial behaviors of empathy, sympathy, helpfulness, cooperation, generosity, nurturing, and caring? Instead of trying to find out whose fault it is when things involving children go wrong, could you have each child look at another child's feelings—then help him to feel better? "Other-esteem conflict conversion" asks children to do that. (See chapter 6: Conflict Conversion.)

When only one child is involved in causing a problem, could the teacher ask the child, "What happened here?" and "What can we do about it?" rather than blaming the child and making him feel shame? Even when the child claims she didn't cause the problem, you could say, "I'm not talking about whose fault it is, but about how we can make things better. Will you help?" Once children feel they are "off the hook" and not being blamed, they are usually quite willing to make things better.

The findings of neuroscientists support this positive approach to child guidance. They warn us against causing emotional stress in young children. They say that a soothing touch, for instance, causes the brain to release growth hormones. Being yelled at or hit, on the other hand, causes the release of the steroid hormone cortisol, high levels of which can cause the death of brain cells as well as a reduction in connections between brain cells important in learning and memory (Newberger, 1997, p. 5).

The kinds of blaming situations you may encounter in the early childhood classroom include:

- Conflicts in which the child who caused a problem is being blamed but denies it.
- Conflicts in which the child who did not cause the problem is being blamed.
- Conflicts in which no one knows who caused the problem.
- Problems reported by someone not involved but being blamed on someone else.

As you can see there is much confusion surrounding "who did it?" You may find yourself responding differently to each of these problems. But should you? Does it really matter who is to blame? If you agree with the premise of this book that conflicts are not bad, but learning opportunities, and that children are not bad, but sometimes need help in resolving conflicts, then you will come to understand that *blame* is not a part of the problem and should not be a part of the solution. *No blame, no shame* should be your motto when it comes to early childhood fault-finding. There are other more effective steps you can take.

STEPS

1. **Have children meet book characters involved in blaming.**
2. **Make funny excuses about "it wasn't my fault."**
3. **Play funny games converting excuses to good feelings.**

ACTIVITIES

1. **Have children meet book characters involved in blaming.**
   - Books with characters who face fault-finding dilemmas can help children learn what they should do (see Figure 14–1). As Koc and Buzzelli (2004) mention:

     Through literature, children can observe other people's lives, experiences, and various versions of moral conflict and learn to take others' perspectives. They can also recognize moral and ethical dilemmas by observing the behavior of story characters. (p. 93)

   - One of the funniest of the "faulty" characters is bumbling Murdley Gurdson, the little boy who is always causing accidents in *It Wasn't My Fault.* One day he goes out for a walk with one shoe on (the other is lost), when someone lays an egg on his head. Thus begins a day of buck-passing of hilarious proportions. The bird that laid the egg blames the screaming of an aardvark, who blames a pygmy hippo that stepped on its tail, who blames a hopping shoe with long ears that turns out to be a hopping rabbit that landed in the shoe and got stuck. Whose shoe was it? Murdley's, of course. On the second reading of the book ask the children why each animal said it wasn't its fault and blamed another animal. How did the animals being blamed feel? Was it any animal's fault? Does it really matter? This is an important question children should consider about their own blaming of others: Does it matter who is at fault? Then ask: What really does matter in these conflicts? Does anyone answer: the other person's feelings?
   - *Who Sank the Boat?* is a fine story for a dramatic reenactment with children taking the roles of the cow, the donkey, the sheep. the pig, and the mouse getting into a pretend boat. As each animal steps gingerly into the boat the narrator asks: Do you know who sank the boat? When the mouse finally gets in, the boat sinks with a terrific splash. (Have all your actors plunk down suddenly.) So who *did* sink it? What will your children say? Do they all agree?

2. **Make funny excuses about "it wasn't my fault."**
   - One of the best books for excuses is *David Gets in Trouble.* When his skateboard knocks over a table in the living room he claims: "I didn't mean to." When his ball goes through a window he says: "It was an accident." When he walks down the street without his pants: "I forgot." Other excuses: "My dog ate my homework." "I couldn't help it." "I was hungry." "But she likes it." "It slipped." "No, it wasn't me." In the end David says: "It was me. I'm sorry."

FIGURE 14–1 Books with Fault-Finding Themes.

Carlos and the Squash Plant (Stevens, 1993)*

David Gets in Trouble (Shannon, 2002)

The Gorilla Did It (Hazen, 1974)

It Wasn't My Fault (Lester, 1985)

Sorry Miss Folio (Furtado, 1992)

Trigwater Did It (Rovetch, 1991)

Who Sank the Boat (Allen, 1982)

Why Mosquitoes Buzz in People's Ears (Aardema, 1975)*

*multicultural

This girl meets Carlos, the boy who makes excuses about washing his ears.

- When you read the story a second time ask children what other excuses David could have made up. Write all these excuses and others you can think of on strips of paper to be used in the next activity.

3. **Play funny games converting excuses to good feelings.**

   - Put several large plastic jars wrapped with colored tissue paper around the classroom and fill them with "good-feelings-words." Write the words on slips of paper or 3 × 5 cards for each jar. For example, words that mean *happy* might include:

glad	overjoyed
joyful	jubilant
cheerful	elated
pleased	delighted
thrilled	tickled

   - Fill the happy jar with numerous copies of these words. Then create other jars wrapped in other colors of tissue paper and fill each with particular good-feelings-words such as *proud, wonderful, funny, exciting.* You'll have to help children read the words and talk about the feelings. Introduce the children to the jars and their colors: happy-red, proud-blue, wonderful-pink, funny-orange, exciting-purple.

   - Next, take the strips of paper and read off each excuse. Children can choose which excuse they want to carry on a march around the room. When everyone is ready play a peppy tune and have children march around the room carrying their excuses. Then stop the music suddenly and have the children stop. Children who are near one of the jars can put their excuses in the jar and take out a happy word. Keep the march going and stopping until all have exchanged their excuses for happy words. Have them say their word and show in a funny way what it means.

   - Another time wrap beanbags with excuse-strips and have children try to toss them into cartons labeled with happy words. What else can you do with fault-finding excuses? Feed them to the dinosaurs in the block center? Wouldn't it be exciting if these children grew up to be adults who didn't blame others?

REFERENCES AND SUGGESTED READINGS

Beaty, J. J. (1995). *Converting conflicts in preschool.* Clifton Park, NY: Thomson Delmar Learning.

Clare, L., & Gillimore, R. (1996). Using moral dilemmas in children's literature as a vehicle for moral education and teaching. *Journal of Moral Education 25*(3), 325–331.

Damon, W. (1988). *The moral child: Nurturing children's natural moral growth.* New York: The Free Press.

Kagan, J. (1984). *The nature of the child.* New York: Basic Books.

Koc, K., & Buzzelli, C. A. (2004). The moral of the story is . . . Using children's literature in moral education. *Young Children, 59*(1), 92–97.

Newberger, J. J. (1997). New brain research: A wonderful window of opportunity to build public support for early childhood education. *Young Children, 52*(4), 4–9.

Children's Books

Aardema, V. (1975). *Why mosquitoes buzz in people's ears.* New York: Dial Books.*

Allen, P. (1982). *Who sank the boat?* New York: Coward-McCann, Inc.

Furtado, J. (1992). *Sorry, Miss Folio.* New York: Kane/Miller.

Hazen, B. S. (1974). *The gorilla did it.* New York: Macmillan.

Lester, H. (1985). *It wasn't my fault.* Boston: Houghton Mifflin.

Rovetch, L. (1991). *Trigwater did it.* New York: Puffin.

Shannon, D. (2002). *David gets in trouble.* New York: Blue Sky Press.

Stevens, J. R. (1993). *Carlos and the squash plant.* Flagstaff, AZ: Northland.*

———

*multicultural

15 FRIENDSHIP

CONCEPT

Friendships in early childhood classrooms are an important factor in the type of interactions among the children as well as the emotional tone of the class. Because young children are at an egocentric stage of their development, they tend to be immersed in their own needs, making conflicts over possessions, space, and turns a common daily occurrence. However, when friends are involved, children are more likely to adjust their needs and either negotiate, compromise, or withdraw from such conflicts (McDevitt & Ormrod, 2004). Children learn from each other how far they can go before others object. Thus friendships between some children are models for other children on how to behave in order to maintain the peace.

Just what are friendships for young children? Ramsey (1991) describes friendships in preschools as "playmateships" in which children think of their most frequent companions as their friends. In other words, friends are the youngsters a child plays with.

> Friendships are defined by the current situation. Children sometimes say "I can't be your friend today" when they really mean "I'm playing with somebody else right now." Because frequency of association is often determined by availability and proximity, some friendship choices may reflect convenience more than personal preference for that particular child. (p. 21)

Many young children do develop a preference for a particular child based on similar play styles and interests. Such relationships are not necessarily as long-lasting as they would be with older children, and may break apart when children's interests change. With the many activities and materials available in most classrooms, friendships may come and go as children shift from one interest to another. Whether or not friendships are stable, they add a conducive element to the emotional tone of the class. They seem to make children more content and engaged in learning activities, while putting a damper on the number of conflicts that might ordinarily occur.

Does this mean it is up to the teacher to promote friendships among the children? Many early childhood educators would argue against it on the basis that such involvement interferes with the children's own social development. Just as children should be allowed to settle many of their own conflicts, so they should be allowed to develop their own friendships if, in fact, this is what they want. On the other hand, there may be some children who are desperate to find a friend, but haven't a clue about how to go about it. "Playing it by ear" may be your best advice: Support those who have friends while assisting those who may need help. In either case it is best not to announce to the class who is friends with whom. The following steps may help:

STEPS

1. **Read several friendship theme books to small groups of children and discuss them.**
2. **Have children draw pictures of friends and dictate stories about them. Imaginary friends are fine.**
3. **Have a "phone day" with one child making a pretend phone call to another.**

ACTIVITIES

1. **Read several friendship theme books to small groups of children and discuss them. Some of the books you might read are listed in Figure 15–1.**

   - Two classic books on friendship in preschool are Cohen's *Will I Have a Friend?* and *Best Friends.* Children enjoy following Jim as he goes with Pa to his first day at preschool, all the while worrying "Will I have a friend?" Pa tells him, "I think you will." Jim looks around at all the other children talking and playing with each other, but he can't see his friend. Then it happens at nap time when Paul on the mat next to him shows Jim a little truck. As you read the book again, ask your listeners what they would have done on each page. *Best Friends* presents the dilemma of who is who's best friend. Jim wants Paul to be his but other children interfere and soon Paul is not speaking to him. A classroom emergency of the light bulb going out in the incubator brings the two boys together again and makes them heroes for saving the eggs. Listen to what your children have to comment on the topic "best friends."

   - In *Jessica* Ruthie Simms has an invisible friend called Jessica who goes everywhere with Ruthie, even to kindergarten. Her parents tell Ruthie, "There is no Jessica." But for Ruthie there is. Then on her first day of school when invisible Jessica wants very badly to go home, a girl comes up to Ruthie and asks to be her partner. Her name turns out to be Jessica, and off they go together. Do any of your children have friends no one but they can see? Will they talk about these friends?

2. **Have children draw pictures of friends and dictate stories about them. Imaginary friends are fine.**

   - One teacher decides to have children draw pictures of themselves and their friends or field trip partners after they take a class trip to pick apples. She reasons that no one should feel left out because they don't have a friend, since everyone on the trip has a partner. The activity takes place after an animated discussion of the trip. Children had been fascinated by the fact that the red apples were ripe and sweet, but the green ones were not ripe but sour. Figures 15–2 and 15–3 are examples of children's drawings. Most of the children (4-year-olds) dictated only a sentence or two about their pictures—more like a caption than a story.

3. **Have a "phone day" with one child making a pretend phone call to another.**

   - Children liked the idea of having a phone day where they made pretend phone calls to "phone friends." They took turns using play phones all day long. The teacher wasn't sure whether this promoted friendships as she hoped, but it surely promoted language development. One boy even got the character doll "Carlos" in the act by speaking for him as he phoned different children.

FIGURE 15–1 Books With Friendship Themes.

> *Being Friends* (Beaumont, 2002)*
>
> *Best Friends* (Cohen, 1971)*
>
> *Four Friends Together* (Heap, 2003)
>
> *Friends* (Lewis, 1997)
>
> *Hunter's Best Friend at School* (Elliott, 2002)
>
> *I'm Calling Molly* (Kurtz, 1990)*
>
> *Jessica* (Henkes, 1989)
>
> *That's What Friends Do* (Cave, 2004)
>
> *Will I Have a Friend?* (Cohen, 1967)*

*multicultural

FIGURE 15–2 Lacey Has the Sour Apple and I Have the Good Red One.

FIGURE 15–3 I Like Green Apples, Bananas, and Plums. My Partner Likes Strawberries.

- Either before or during phone day read *I'm Calling Molly* (Kurtz, 1990): how Christopher phones his friend Molly next door, only to find that Molly won't play with him because she is playing dress-up with Rebekah. Finally Rebekah's mother comes and picks her up. Now Christopher doesn't need to call Molly over and over because Molly's calling him. Ask children what they would do.

On phone day this boy spoke on the phone for the Carlos character doll.

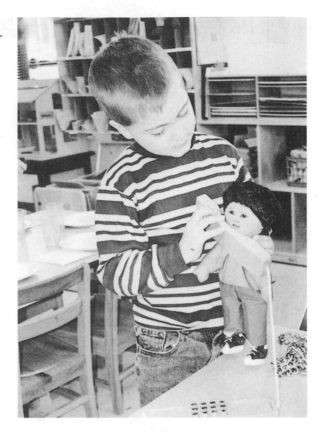

REFERENCES AND SUGGESTED READINGS

Burton, R. A., & Denham, S. A. (1998). "Are you my friend?" How young children learn to get along with others. *Journal of Research in Early Childhood. 12,* 210–224.

Corsaro, W. (1981). Social organization in peer environment. In S. R. Asher & I. M Gottman (Eds.), *The development of children's friendships.* New York: Cambridge University Press.

Howes, C. (1996). The earliest friendships. In W. M. Bukowski, A. F. Newcomb, & W. W. Hartup (Eds.), *The company they keep: Friendships in childhood and adolescence.* New York: Cambridge University Press.

Kemple, K. M. (1991). Preschool children's peer acceptance and social interactions. *Young Children, 46*(5), 47–54.

McDevitt, T. M., & Ormrod, J. E. (2004). *Child development: Educating and working with children and adolescents.* Upper Saddle River, NJ: Merrill/Prentice Hall.

Ramsey, P. G. (1991). *Making friends in school: Promoting peer relationships in early childhood.* New York: Teachers College Press.

Children's Books

Beaumont, K. (2002). *Being friends.* New York: Dial.*

Cave, K. (2004). *That's what friends do.* New York: Hyperion.

Cohen, M. (1967). *Will I have a friend?* New York: Collier Books.*

Cohen, M. (1971). *Best friends.* New York: Collier Books.*

Elliott, L. M. (2002). *Hunter's best friend at school.* New York: HarperCollins.

Heap, S. (2003). *Four friends together.* Cambridge, MA: Candlewick Press.

Henkes, K. (1989). *Jessica.* New York: Puffin Books.

Kurtz, J. (1990). *I'm calling Molly.* Morton Grove, IL: Albert Whitman.*

Lewis, K. (1997). *Friends.* Cambridge, MA: Candlewick Press.

---

*multicultural

16 GENEROSITY

CONCEPT

Generosity means being liberal in giving and sharing things. In early childhood programs it applies both to children and especially to their teachers. Think about yourself. Are you generous in what you give to the children? You may feel that most of your time is devoted to them. But research about how frequently preschool teachers interact with individual children shows just the opposite. One study, in fact, showed that 31% of the children in Head Start, child care, and preschool classrooms received no individual attention during the researchers' observations. In 12% of those classrooms more than half of the children received no individual attention at all (Lazer, Goodson, & Moss, 1993).

Saying "hello" in the morning is not enough. What happens during the rest of the day? Do you read books to individuals, give hugs, give compliments, help them get started on a project, play with them on the playground, choose them to be a leader, do a puzzle together, talk with them at lunch time, ask them to help you with a task, have them show you what they accomplished, take a picture of them, call them on a toy telephone, ask about their lives and how they are feeling—every day?

Think about it. Are you really reaching every single child in your class? Kontos & Wilcox-Herzog (1997) looked at what drew teachers to give time to certain children.

> Teachers interact more frequently with children who seek adult contact, whose behavior requires frequent intervention, who spend more time in activities that require adult assistance, and who are personally more appealing to the individual teacher. (p. 5)

Their further findings indicated that preschool children were more competent in their own peer interactions when they had more frequent responsive involvement with their teachers. This result seems to be saying that when teachers give more attention to each child, their behavior with their peers improves. If this is truly the case, you need to make certain you are reaching each child in your class on a daily basis.

Reread chapter 3: Attention-Seeking for ideas about some of the activities you can do with individuals. That particular strategy addressed attention-seeking children. But it is just as important that you give as much of your attention and time as possible to every child, every day. A tall order, you may think, when you have 15 to 20 children in the class. But you also have staff members who can help. Here are some ideas.

STEPS

1. **Give an animal sticker to every child every day for something he/she accomplishes.**
2. **Stamp each child's hand with one of your stampers.**
3. **Have children read about, talk about gift-giving and receiving.**

ACTIVITIES

1. Give an animal sticker to every child every day for something he/she accomplishes.

- Here is one way you can tell if every child has been attended to personally. If he or she is not wearing a sticker by the end of the day you can give him one along with a hug. What does he need to accomplish? Anything. Something he does, something he says, or just for coming to school that day. Thank him and compliment him, then ask him to choose his sticker to wear for that day. Can he tell you why he chose that particular sticker?

2. Stamp each child's hand with one of your stampers.

- Go around to children one by one and ask them a guessing-game question such as "Guess what I have in my hand?" No matter what their answer, tell them you are stamping the hands of everyone who answered your question. Use different stampers every day—with washable ink, of course. Can they tell what the stamp is? Constructive Playthings (1–800–448–4115) has alphabet letters, bug, dinosaur, transportation, farm, sea life, and wild animal stampers.

- Have a brief conversation with each child and get to know him or her. You will be giving them your attention and they will be sharing something from their lives.

- After you have completed a week of your giving to individuals, see if it makes a difference in the way children behave toward one another and toward you. You, of course, have been modeling this giving behavior for the children. If you find that conflicts have declined and prosocial behavior has increased, you can begin to involve each child as an assistant giver to go around with you and help with the giving. Giving individual attention and spreading generosity should make your classroom a happy place to be. Even more important, according to Hearron & Hildebrand (2005): "Patterns of prosocial behavior emerging in early childhood are likely to persist into adulthood" (p. 112).

The teacher gives a sticker to a child.

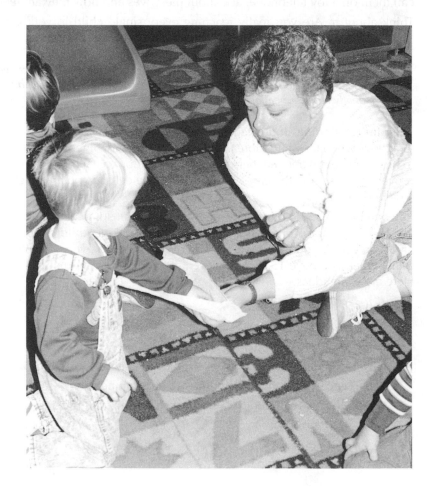

FIGURE 16–1 Books About
Giving and Receiving.

> *Alejandro's Gift* (Albert, 1994)*
>
> *A Birthday Basket for Tia* (Mora, 1992)*
>
> *Fernando's Gift* (Keister, 1995)*
>
> *New Shoes for Silvia* (Hurwitz, 1993)*
>
> *Pablo's Tree* (Mora, 1994)*

*multicultural

3. **Have children read about, talk about gift-giving and receiving.**

   - What can children learn about improving their own generosity? Many teachers start with reading books with gift-giving themes to small groups or individuals. Young children understand about gifts, but mostly about receiving them rather than giving them. Figure 16–1 identifies some rather unusual books about giving and receiving gifts, all involving Hispanic characters.

   - *Alejandro's Gift* tells the story about an old man who lives by himself in the Arizona desert. He is so lonely he uses his time to plant a garden. Then a ground squirrel sneaks up while he is working to take a sip of water from one of the irrigation furrows. Soon all kinds of little desert creatures begin coming: jackrabbits, pocket mice, roadrunners, kangaroo rats, cactus wrens, and even an old desert tortoise. He realizes they are all coming for the water he provides with his windmill. But the big animals won't come—until he digs a water hole for them away from his house. Then, one by one, they come too: a coyote, a badger, a fox, some peccaries, and even a mule deer with fawns. Now he is no longer lonely. Then he understands it was not just a gift he gave them but also a gift he received. Ask your children what were these gifts? What gifts could they give to any wild animals?

   - Would they like to set up a desert scene in their sandbox with a dish of water for the water hole? Have them each draw a desert animal on stiff paper, cut it out, and stand it in the sandbox. They can do a reenactment of the story or make up their own story. If you have an extra paperback copy of the book, you can cut out the man and animal characters and paste them on cardboard for a more realistic reenactment. Children will want the tall saguaro tree cactuses in their desert, too.

   - What can you give to someone who has given so much to you, when you don't have anything? In *A Birthday Basket for Tia,* Cecilia gathers objects that represent memories of the things her Aunt Tia has done for her: a bowl, a teacup, a flowerpot, and a favorite book, and puts them in a basket. Her aunt loves it and treasures each gift. Can your children think of objects they would put in a birthday basket for someone to represent memories of things that person has done for them (perhaps for a grandmother or grandfather)?

   - *Fernando's Gift* (Keister, 1995) in English and Spanish takes place in Costa Rica where Fernando lives with his family; they are involved in planting trees and caring for the rainforest. What can he give his friend Carmina for her birthday? When he learns that Carmina's favorite cristobal tree has been cut down, he decides to give her a small cristobal tree from his father's nursery if he does some chores for his father. Can a tree be a gift? Would your children like to give a tree to someone—maybe the school?

   - *New Shoes for Silvia* takes place in Central America where Silvia lives when she receives a gift from her Aunt Rosita in America: a beautiful pair of red shoes. When she puts them on, she discovers they are too big. She needs to put them away and wait till she grows bigger. But instead she plays with them as doll beds for two dolls, a red train, two red oxen, and a container for shells. Then one day she tries them on again and they fit! What could Silvia do to thank her aunt?

   - *Pablo's Tree* is the story of an adopted boy and his grandfather, who plants a birthday tree the day Pablo's mother brings him home. Every birthday thereafter he hangs a surprise decoration on the tree: paper streamers, colored balloons, paper lanterns, paper bird cages, and finally bells and chimes. Simple but original gifts. You may want to bring a live tree (or limb with branches) into the classroom for a birthday tree. What could the children hang on it for each birthday? Ask the children how they feel about giving gifts. Receiving gifts. Does one make them feel better than the other?

REFERENCES AND SUGGESTED READINGS

Beaty, J. J. (1999). *Prosocial guidance for the preschool child.* Upper Saddle River, NJ: Merrill/Prentice Hall.

Hearron, P. F., & Hildebrand, V. (2005). *Guiding young children* (7th ed.). Upper Saddle River, NJ: Merrill/Prentice Hall.

Kontos, L., & Wilcox-Herzog, A. (1997). Teachers' interactions with children: Why are they so important? *Young Children, 52*(2), 4–12.

Lazer, J. B., & Moss, M. (1993). *Observational study of early childhood programs: Final report, Vol. 1: Life in preschool.* Washington, DC: U.S. Department of Education.

Children's Books

Albert, R. E. (1994). *Alejandro's gift.* San Francisco: Chronicle Books.*

Hurwitz, J. (1993). *New shoes for Silvia.* New York: Morrow Junior Books.*

Keister, D. (1995). *Fernando's gift.* San Francisco: Sierra Club.*

Mora, P. (1992). *A birthday basket for Tia.* New York: Simon & Schuster.*

Mora, P. (1994). *Pablo's tree.* New York: Simon & Schuster.*

---

*multicultural

17 GUIDANCE

CONCEPT

Guidance, or rather the positive guidance described in this text, is a classroom management technique for teachers. It helps young children learn to control their own behavior while developing the prosocial behaviors of self-esteem, other-esteem, friendliness, generosity, cooperation, helpfulness, and respect. In other words, it is a process that you as a teacher can use to help children learn appropriate behavior.

Some teachers already use this technique while others need to learn how it works. As mentioned in chapter 4: Inappropriate Behavior, positive guidance does not look for who's to blame for "bad" behavior, nor does it employ discipline as punishment. Instead, it focuses on: How does the child involved in disruptive behavior feel? What would make her feel better?

Positive guidance is based on research findings about how the brain develops in young children. These findings are used to determine how teachers should react to children's behavior. As Nash (1997) reports:

> Among the first circuits the brain constructs are those that govern emotions. Beginning around two months of age, the distress and contentment experienced by newborns start to evolve into more complex feelings: joy and sadness, envy and empathy, pride and shame. (p. 5)

This brain development continues in early childhood as a child interacts with parents and caregivers. Children begin to learn what's good and what's bad, what's right and what's wrong by the way they are treated—both at home and in the classroom. As Newberger (1997) tells us:

> A child's environment has enormous impact on how the circuits of the brain will be laid . . . Positive interactions with caring adults stimulate a child's brain profoundly, causing synapses to grow and existing connectors to be strengthened. (p. 5)

Thus, it is up to the teachers and staff of an early childhood program to treat every child with respect and not rush to judgment. If she has done something unacceptable, she can learn about it in a calm and nonjudgmental way. One of the teachers' principal tasks is to help children learn appropriate behavior. This is not accomplished through loud voices, harsh treatment, or punishment. It is learned through respect for the child as a person who needs help in learning how to behave. It is learned by allowing the child to work through her feelings. She may be confused, upset, or angry. She may be able to work through these feelings by talking to a teacher who is willing to listen.

When she realizes she is not being blamed or punished, she may feel good enough about herself to tell the teacher how she feels and what would help her feel better. If not, the teacher can suggest a simple activity: reading a book, making a puzzle, painting a picture, or listening to a music tape. If none of these appeal, she may agree to retreat to a quiet nook until she feels better. This is positive guidance. Here are some steps you can use when employing it with a single child who acts inappropriately.

STEPS

1. **Ask the child what is happening; listen attentively.**
2. **Ask the child how she feels; encourage her to express her feelings.**
3. **Ask the child what would help her feel better; make suggestions.**

ACTIVITIES

1. Ask the child what is happening; listen attentively.

- Get down to the child's eye level and talk to her in a quiet voice about what is happening. If she tries to talk about blame—that someone else did something, or that she didn't do it—tell her you are not talking about blame, just wondering what is happening. Say that you heard some shouting and wondered what it was about. Accept whatever she says about it.

- If she doesn't feel like talking, put on a hand puppet and ask her to tell your puppet what the commotion was about. She can whisper if she wants.

- If she still doesn't want to talk to you, will she talk into the microphone of a tape recorder? Tell her nobody can hear what she says but the tape. She can whisper and say anything she wants, and only the tape will hear her.

- Will she talk into a toy phone with you listening on another toy phone?

2. Ask the child how she feels; encourage her to express her feelings.

- Ask how she feels. Try to get her to express her emotions in words. Sometimes the child will cry. You can tell her that tears are okay, that sometimes they make us feel better.

- Maybe she would rather tell your puppet how she feels. Or she could put on a puppet and have her puppet talk to yours; or talk into the tape recorder or a toy phone.

3. Ask the child what would help her feel better; make suggestions.

- By now the child may be able to talk more openly and tell you what would make her feel better. If you know the child, you may already know what her favorite things are. Does she have a stuffed animal she likes to play with? A toy car? She could take her toy to one of the private areas and play with it for awhile until she feels like joining the group again.

- You could set up a new puzzle for her on a floor mat or give her some new doll house figures to play with. Or maybe she wants to write or draw in her journal. Give her a chance to answer after you have made your suggestions.

- Play it by ear. At some point later you can talk to her about classroom limits and appropriate behavior. Be sure to ask for her input, too.

Get down to the child's eye level and talk to her about what is happening.

REFERENCES AND SUGGESTED READINGS

Beaty, J. J. (1999). *Prosocial guidance for the preschool child.* Upper Saddle River, NJ: Merrill/Prentice Hall.

Gartrell, D. (2002). Replacing time-out: Part two—Using guidance to maintain an encouraging classroom. *Young Children, 57*(2), 36–43.

Greenspan, S. I. (1997). *The growth of the mind and the endangered origins of intelligence.* Reading, MA: Addison-Wesley.

Nash, J. M. (1997). Fertile minds. *Time, 149*(5), 48–56.

Newberger, J. J. (1997). New brain development research: A wonderful window of opportunity to build public support for early childhood education. *Young Children, 52*(4), 4–9.

18 HELPFULNESS

CONCEPT

Helpfulness is one of the prosocial behaviors that most young children are very familiar with. They already have to help out at home and also at school. Nevertheless, helping can be featured on particular days so that everyone is aware of its importance in life. Things would not work very well in the world without helpers. What helpers do your children know about? Community helpers such as fire fighters, police officers, bus drivers, crossing guards, mail carriers, nurses, and doctors are some they should be familiar with. What about teachers? Are they community helpers, too?

Can anyone be a helper? Doing a task or helping someone with a task is one way anyone can help. Ask the children how they help out at home. This can be the time to set up a "helpers chart" for classroom chores. There are many other opportunities for children to be involved in helping. Think of the projects you will be setting up and be sure to include children helpers. After they have helped are there ways for them to record their contributions?

Helping is a two-way street. That means it includes teachers helping children, too. When children ask you to help them, should you do it? You will need to use your judgment. Young children should be encouraged to do as much as they can on their own to learn new skills and solve their own problems. For example, if they can't zip up a jacket, should you do it for them? It is better if you show them how and hold the jacket for them to do it by themselves. Children become too dependent on adults who do everthing for them.

On the other hand, some children become very upset when they can't make things work the way they should. With a puzzle maker who gives up before he really gets started, you can best help by sitting next to him and handing him a piece to try. If he can't fit it anywhere, show him how to turn it around until it fits. Stay with him unitl he finishes.

Sometimes cleanup is too overwhelming for the children who have taken all the blocks off the shelves. You can help by demonstrating ways to make it more interesting, such as using a large block as a bulldozer to push smaller blocks over to the shelves, or pretending to feed the blocks to the hungry dinosaur who lives on the shelves. Your best help may be just being there watching, encouraging, and cheering them on.

After help has been given it is important to thank the helpers. If you serve as a model and thank children for helping, they can be encouraged to thank you and others.

STEPS

1. **Set up a helpers chart for classroom chores.**
2. **Have a "helping day" where children read about, talk about, and do helping.**
3. **Have children record their helping in the pictures they draw.**
4. **Have children find ways to thank people who have helped them.**

ACTIVITIES

1. **Set up a helpers chart for classroom chores.**
   - Be sure to encourage children's input when you decide what classroom tasks children can be involved in and what names you will use for the helpers. Children enjoy having special titles with a badge or some kind of identifying bracelet, necklace, or sign. One class chose the name "attendant" to designate the helpers. Here are their categories:

Animal Attendants	**Book Attendants**
Feed and water guinea pigs	Help with book signup and return
Feed fish	**Weather Attendants**
Attendance Attendants	Check on kind of weather
Help take attendance	Mark weather chart
Mark attendance chart	**Plant Attendants**
Food Attendants	Water plants
Help set tables	Measure and record growth
Fold napkins	**Supplies Attendants**
Nap Attendants	Put paint at easels
Help set up and put away cots	Help set up activity tables
Help get out blankets	

   Did you laugh about "attendance attendants" like the children did? Also there was some controversy over "book attendants" who wanted to be called "librarians."

2. **Have a "helping day" where children read about, talk about, and do helping.**
   - Some helping days are set up in conjunction with projects the class is involved with. One class took on a gardening project that led the whole group to become gardeners. First they read about planting from some of the books in Figure 18–1. Then they divided up the various helping tasks. Some went with the teacher to buy seeds and plants. Some prepared the soil; some planted the seeds and transplanted tomato plants; some watered the plants; some made signs for the things they had planted.
   - The children loved hearing the Carlos books read in both English and Spanish about the Hispanic boy who helped his father plant, but was always getting into some kind of ethical dilemma: not telling his mother the truth about washing his ears, and not telling his father how he planted the cornfield wrong. They were determined to plant their garden right and wash carefully afterward.

3. **Have children record their helping in the pictures they draw.**
   - In this rural area many classes had children who were involved in helping their families with their gardens. They were encouraged to draw pictures of their helping and tell stories about

FIGURE 18–1 Books with a Gardening Theme.

> *Flower Garden* (Bunting, 1994)*
>
> *Planting a Rainbow* (Ehlert, 1988)
>
> *Carlos and the Cornfield* (Stevens, 1995)*
>
> *Carlos and the Squash Plant* (Stevens, 1993)*

*multicultural

Some children help the teacher prepare the soil for their garden.

Other children help water the garden.

FIGURE 18–2 I Love to Help My Mom Make Healthy Food. I Help Wash All the Fruits and Vegetables.

FIGURE 18–3 This Is Me Raking Grandpa's Garden.

their pictures. A calendar was made from some of the pictures. Figures 18–2 and 18–3 are two examples.

4. **Have children find ways to thank people who have helped them.**

   • Depending on who helped them and what was done, children in various classrooms developed creative ways of thanking their helpers. For the garden store that provided seeds and plants, the children dictated a thank-you note that everyone signed. They also sent along one of their calendars.

   • Other ideas for thank-you's included: making a tape in which each child says a sentence as well as thanks; making a wall mural and having everyone sign it; taking photos of their garden when full grown and sending them with a thank-you note; inviting the helpers to the class to share a tomato salad from their tomato plants.

When every child is involved in exciting projects like this, fewer conflicts than normal arise. Children all have particular chores; they learn to share, to take turns, to wait for a turn, and to thank those who have helped them. Best of all they feel good about their contributions in helping to make a successful garden.

REFERENCES AND SUGGESTED READINGS

Beaty, J. J. (1999). *Prosocial guidance for the preschool child.* Upper Saddle River, NJ: Merrill/Prentice Hall.

Children's Books
Bunting, E. (1994). *Flower garden.* San Diego: Harcourt.*
Ehlert, L. (1988). *Planting a rainbow.* San Diego: Harcourt.
Stevens, J. R. (1993). *Carlos and the squash plant.* Flagstaff, AZ: Rising Moon.*
Stevens, J. R. (1995). *Carlos and the cornfield.* Flagstaff, AZ: Rising Moon.*

———

*multicultural

19 HITTING, BITING

CONCEPT

The inappropriate behaviors of hitting and biting did not start out that way. Biting seems to be an impulsive act. Most children go through a period of biting their caregivers during their first year, according to Brazelton and Sparrow (2001). It seems to be more exploratory than aggressive, and is generally stopped by caregivers without much of a fuss. But some children continue using biting during their second year, perhaps to get the caregiver's attention. Then they bite another child, which results in screaming on the part of the bitten child and violent reactions from the parents. This overreaction may surprise and even overwhelm the biter. But she may try it again to see if she gets the same reaction. Brazelton and Sparrow continue:

> *Any implusive behavior such as biting or hurting is frightening to the child. She doesn't know how to stop. She repeats it over and over as if she were trying to find out why it produces such a powerful response. Biting, scratching, and hitting all start out as normal exploratory behaviors. When adults overreact or disregard the behavior, the child will repeat the behavior as if to say, "I'm out of control. Help me!"* (p. 49)

As a teacher in an early childhood program you must, of course, stop such behavior, but do it in a way that is quick, firm, and to the point—not harsh, blaming, and punishing. It may mean you must hold the child firmly or take her to one side telling her you don't allow children to hurt other children. Say this in a firm but matter-of-fact way. You must do this every time this impulsive behavior occurs in order to break the cycle of a child being out of control. But you and she must also have in mind an immediate substitute behavior she can resort to once she has calmed down. The ultimate goal is to help the child learn to stop herself.

STEPS

1. **Stop the biting or hitting immediately.**
2. **Give the child a substitute material to bite or hit.**
3. **Talk with the child and read to her about the actions of other children who need to control their feelings.**

ACTIVITIES

1. **Stop the biting or hitting immediately.**

   - This is not a conflict conversion situation, as such. It involves stopping this impulsive and dangerous action itself. If you act quickly and firmly but not punatively, you should be able to stop this habitual response that is damaging to all concerned.

   - Tell the child no one is allowed to hurt another child in the class. Say it firmly but calmly. Keep anger out of your voice. Tell her you will help her find something else to bite that won't hurt anyone. Be sure your face does not register anger.

2. **Give the child a substitute material to bite or hit.**

- With children who bite, think of a material that involves the mouth. When the child is calm enough, talk to him about how he feels when he wants to bite. What could he bite on whenever he feels that same way? Some children mention a rubber ball or some other rubber toy. You might suggest a rubber animal stamper such as a tiger or a shark. You could punch a hole through the stamper and string it on a yarn cord that the child could wear around his neck. Then when he felt like biting, he could bite on it.

- Another child told the teacher she blew bubbles. The teacher wasn't sure what this meant, so the girl described how her mother put water in a plastic container and squeezed a few drops of dish detergent in the water. Then she gave her a plastic straw to blow on and make bubbles. It certainly made sense, using the negative energy from her mouth in this manner by blowing away all the anger. Did she make a lot of bubbles, the teacher wondered? Sometimes she blew enough to overflow on the floor, the girl replied.

- What about hitting? What could an out-of-control child hit to release such strong anger energy? With children who hit, think of a material that involves the hands. Some children suggested punching pillows, and the teacher agreed. Others mentioned punching an inflated clown, but the teacher felt that looked too much like hitting a person and rejected the idea. She suggested instead filling a sponge with water, placing it in a shallow dry pan, and punching the water out of it. It could make quite a mess if the sponge was a big one, but that could remind the child of how much angry energy flew around when he hit someone.

3. **Talk with the child and read to her about the actions of other children who need to control their feelings.**

- Talk with the children who are trying different substitute materials to help control their anger. Is it working? Do they need to continue with the materials or would they like to try something different? Would they like to meet some book characters who also hit or bite?

- Hitting and biting are not always impulsive acts. Sometime they are done by bullies who try to dominate other children by threatening or harming them. In *Bootsie Barker Bites* (Bottner,

This girl blew bubbles into soapy water when she became upset.

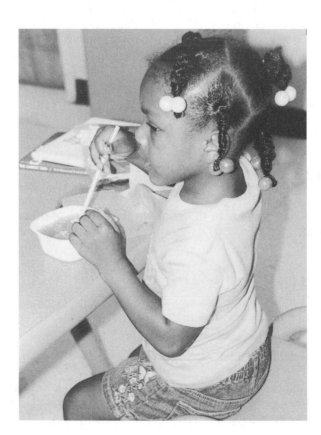

1992), when Bootsie visits the little girl narrator's bedroom to play, she pushes the girl around and threatens to eat her alive because she is a dinosaur. The little girl is terrified until her mother tells her to play a different game with Bootsie. Next time Bootsie finds that the girl is a paleontologist with a trowel in her hand ready to dig up dinosaur bones. Bootsie turns and runs.

• When Katie Honor in *Sometimes I'm Bombaloo* (Vail, 2002) loses her temper at home she uses her feet and fists instead of words. She scatters toys and hits her little brother. Her mother sends her to her room, but she still yells and throws things until something funny happens and then she becomes Katie Honor again. Humor can actually cure (see Chapter 20: Humor).

REFERENCES AND SUGGESTED READINGS

Beaty, J. J. (2006). *Observing development of the young child.* Upper Saddle River, NJ: Merrill/Prentice Hall.

Brazelton, T. B., & Sparrow, J. D. (2001). *Touchpoints three to six: Your child's emotional and behavioral development.* Cambridge, MA: Perseus Publishing.

Wolfson-Steinberg, L. (2000). "He hit me!" "She pushed me!" Where does is start? How can it stop? *Young Children, 55*(3), 38–42.

Children's Books

Bottner, B. (1992). *Bootsie Baker bites.* New York: G. P. Putnam's Sons.

Vail, R. (2002). *Sometimes I'm Bombaloo.* New York: Scholastic Press.

20 HUMOR

CONCEPT

Why should "humor" be a strategy in a guidance textbook? Mark Twain will tell you: "Against the assault of laughter, nothing can stand!" If you can laugh, you can get over anything. Laughter has real power to affect the human brain and body. When you laugh, the brain releases enzymes that make you feel good. How young children react to humor is explained by Brazelton & Sparrow (2001):

> Humor depends on the cognitive capacity to compare and store memories and develop a general
> sense of what usually happens. Then the child must be able to compare the immediate situation to
> his understanding of what usually happens. For a child, the fun of nonsense is the satisfaction he feels
> in knowing that he can tell the difference between what makes sense and what doesn't.
> (pp. 389–390)

Humor in an early childhood classroom can be used to diffuse a tense situation. Someone can make a joke, say something silly, sing a funny song, or act in a silly manner. Humor can help children settle down and return to normal. When things get too loud the teacher can say even louder: HILDA MUST BE DANCING! Children know at once she is referring to a much-loved book where Hilda Hippo dances the flamenco in her favorite pair of heels, and bananas fall in gooey heaps, shaken from their peels. The children must then shake themselves, fall down in gooey heaps—and emit peals of laughter.

A classroom where the teacher can laugh—with the children, and even at herself—is a classroom where children can feel free to be themselves. Nonsensical things make children laugh: Silly Sally going to town walking backwards upside down; Murdley Gurdson going around with an egg on his head; a porcupine with a name like Fluffy. Nonsensical words make children laugh: "oonga boonga," "Oliver Boliver Butt," "squelches when it walks." Say them to your children and see what happens. When children laugh together, their anger disappears; their sadness is lifted; their fears are dissipated. We need to lighten up and laugh like children do. We do not use humor as much as we should. It is truly a magical ingredient in positive guidance.

STEPS

1. **Have a drop-in-and-laugh time in a different learning center every day.**
2. **When two children are arguing use humor to lighten the situation.**
3. **When children have to do something scary (like go to the dentist) have them practice it humorously ahead of time.**

ACTIVITIES

1. **Have a drop-in-and-laugh time in a different learning center every day.**
   - What will be the funny activity today? Children can hardly wait to come into the classroom when you have a drop-in-and-laugh time. Put up a drop-in-and-laugh sign in a particular center and have some funny activity that four children at a time can choose during free-choice time.

This girl got the baby to stop crying by saying: "Hokey, smokey, you're too pokey."

- **ART.** Have the area set up ahead of time with posters showing planets, space ships, and the night sky. Have three bowls of colored play dough (red, yellow, and green) ready for the children to make their own aliens. Have a basket of odds and ends to stick onto the aliens for protuberances and eyeballs. Read the book *Here Come the Aliens* (McNaughton, 1995) about the bizarre-looking aliens who squelch when they walk and grunt and burp and squeak. The aliens are coming from outer space (are you scared?), but when they get close to Earth they see a picture that changes their minds. It is a bunch of kids aged four. It scares them off—away they roar. The aliens are going! Children love to laugh all through it.

- **DRAMATIC PLAY.** Another day, have this center set up for housekeeping as it usually is, only have a baby doll in a basket or cradle waiting for someone to comfort it with a funny word. Can you play a tape of a baby crying? If not, make the sounds yourself after you have read the book *Oonga Boonga* (Wishinsky, 1998) about Baby Louise. Nobody could stop her crying until her brother Daniel came and said oonga boonga. Have the baby cry several times and have different children try to stop her with silly words or actions. It is up to you to stop and start her again for the next person to try. Are the children laughing too hard to say their words?

- **MUSIC.** In this center play loud booming music and beat on a drum to attract four children at a time. Then read them *Hilda Must Be Dancing* (Wilson, 2004) about the hippo who dances so hard the jungle floor quakes like a tidal wave. Have different children choose to be Hilda, who pounds the floor as she dances and twirls around as you read the book. Are they laughing yet?

2. **When two children are arguing use humor to lighten the situation.**

- Choose one of the books with rhyming, nonsensical verses that children love and read from it in a whispery tone into the ear of each arguer. See how long it takes for them to start laughing. For instance, children in one class loved *Trout, Trout, Trout!* (Sayre, 2004) and went into hysterical laughter whenever it was read because of the hilarious-sounding names of the fish: "Shovelnose Sturgeon/ love that face/ Spoonhead Sculpin/ Dace, Dace, Dace!"

- Make up your own crazy verses and use them the same way. But don't use real children's names.

Bailey's in a tailspin,	Come, come, come,	What's your rush, rush, rush,
Belda's in a tizzy,	Little dum-diddle-dum,	Through the crush, crush, crush,
Bork is singing la-di-da,	Let us run, run, run,	While we gush, gush, gush,
Cause he's getting dizzy.	For the fun-fiddle-fun.	Over mush, mush, mush?
		Yum! (or Yuck!)

3. **When children have to do something scary (like go to the dentist) have them practice it humorously ahead of time.**

- Set up your dramatic play center as a dentist's office with a cushioned chair, a table, and a lamp next to it. Put tools from the woodworking center on the table (pliers, saw, hammer, drill). Have paper cups with colored water to rinse, and a basin to spit in. Have stickers ready to give to each patient. The children in the center can sit in the row of chairs against the wall while awaiting their turn in the chair. Have the dentist wear a white jacket. (A long-sleeve white shirt worn backwards is fine.) Once a child is in the chair read one of the following books. The waiting children can be characters in the stories. Give them head bands, name cards on necklaces, animal ears, or face masks.

- Read *Open Wide* (Barber, 2004) about Sam Spurr who is so afraid he hides under the dentist's chair. The dentist squeezes under too and works on him there while telling tales of the animals whose teeth he has worked on: a tiger with a mouse tail stuck in his back teeth; a nanny goat who needed new false teeth; a hippo with a toothache (he gave Sam the tooth he pulled); a beaver whose teeth were blunt; a crocodile with babies who came for a checkup (all of the babies wanted the same sticker); a toucan with a twisted beak; a whale attacked by hammerhead sharks; and a spitting cobra. You know what your children will like best (after laughing). Rinsing and spitting! They can each do it and then get their sticker.

- In *Harry and the Dinosaurs Say "Raahh!"* (Whybrow, 2001), Harry gets all his dinosaurs in his bucket and his mother rides off with him on her bicycle to the dentist. Harry doesn't want to get in the chair so the dentist offers one of his dinosaurs a turn. Harry presses his magic button and the tyrannosaurus grows very big. That scares the dentist so Harry makes him little again. He climbs into the chair with his bucket of dinosaurs and they all open their mouths and say "Raahh!" The dinosaurs love the rinsing and spitting. Have your waiting children each hold a plastic dinosaur for their turn.

REFERENCES AND SUGGESTED READINGS

Beaty, J. J. (2004). *Skills for preschool teachers.* Upper Saddle River, NJ: Merrill/Prentice Hall.

Brazelton, T. B., & Sparrow, J. D. (2001). *Touchpoints three to six: Your child's emotional and behavioral development.* Cambridge, MA: Perseus Publishing.

Children's Books

Barber, T. (2004). *Open wide.* London: Chrysalis Children's Books (distributed by Publishers Group West).

McNaughton, C. (1995). *Here come the aliens.* Cambridge, MA: Candlewick Press.

Sayre, A. P. (2004). *Trout, trout, trout! A fish chant.* Chanhassen, MN: NorthWord Press.

Whybrow, I. (2001). *Harry and the dinosaurs say "raahh!"* New York: Random House.

Wilson, K. (2004). *Hilda must be dancing.* New York: Margaret K. McElderry Books.

Wishinsky, F. (1998). *Oonga boonga.* New York: Dutton's Children's Books.

(Books are available in Barnes & Noble stores, online at amazon.com, and in libraries.)

21 INTERVENTION

CONCEPT

Teachers need to intervene in children's inappropriate behavior when there is hitting, biting, name-calling, or hurting—when things are out-of-control. These are actions the teacher must stop quickly. But teachers themselves should not get upset, for they need to realize that these times are learning times for the children—just what children came into the program to do: learn appropriate behavior. Difficult as it may seem, you can help make a big difference in the lives of such children.

It is often only one or two children in the group who act out like this. Most of the children have learned how to deal with conflicts on their own or by following the conflict conversion technique you have shown them (see chapter 6: Conflict Conversion). Nevertheless, it is essential for you to find ways to help these other children learn appropriate behavior. They are actually giving you the opportunity to change the direction they are taking. What they learn may last them all their lives. Here are steps you can take.

STEPS

1. **When you intervene remain calm and unruffled.**
2. **Move quickly to the site of the out-of-control behavior and halt it.**
3. **Calm the child by remaining with him.**
4. **Help the child to verbalize what happened.**
5. **Direct the child to a calming activity.**
6. **Talk with the other children involved.**

ACTIVITIES

1. **When you intervene remain calm and unruffled.**

   - Most important in this interaction is *how* you intervene. Intervention should be done calmly but decisively without exaggerating the situation. Attention-seeking children will repeat their actions to get you to react out-of-control yourself. They are used to having adults become upset at their actions since this is their principal way of gaining attention. If you can keep your cool when they have caused a major disruption, you are showing them things are not all that bad. You are in control of your behavior just as they can be in control of theirs, too. As Greenspan (1997) notes:

     To feel secure, they must believe that adults will help them keep their anger, greed, frustration, and other negative emotions in check. This must be done, however, through positive means that impose rigor yet protect the child's self-esteem. (p. 224)

2. **Move quickly to the site of the out-of-control behavior and halt it.**

   - Do not call out across the room for the child to stop. That only disturbs everyone else. Keep emotional outbursts as private and contained as possible. It is not the other children's business. They can go on with their own activities. Instead, move quickly to the out-of-control child and move him away from the others. You may have to physically contain him by putting an arm around him or leading him by the arm. If he is kicking, you may need to remove his shoes. You can hold him until he calms down.

3. **Calm the child by remaining with him.**

   - Talk quietly in low tones, telling him: "Calm down, Andre, calm down, calm down. It's all right now. I'm going to hold you until you feel better. Let me know when you feel better." When you feel the child relax, ask him if he feels better now. If he doesn't answer, he is probably not ready for you to let him go. If your center has an adult rocking chair, you can hold him in the chair and rock. Otherwise, sit with him in a private spot, perhaps on floor pillows or a beanbag chair. This is not the time to make a child sit in a "time-out chair" in isolation from everyone. He needs you to be nearby, and he needs to know that he is not being punished, but calmed down. It is important to have a comfortable private retreat like this if you have children in the program who lose control easily.

4. **Help the child to verbalize what happened.**

   - When the child is finally calm enough, have him tell you what happened. You have time to wait for him to do this. The other staff can be working with other children. You may need to get him started with lead questions. "What happened Andre?" "Yes, I saw those boys teasing you, but now we're talking about feelings, and not whose fault it is." Keep the topic focused on feelings and not blame. What can he tell you about his feelings? Is he angry? Does he feel like there's a knot inside him that wants to explode? Listen to his remarks impartially without blaming or shaming him or any of the others.

5. **Direct the child to a calming activity.**

   - If he does not want to be held after he has regained control, let him sit in the chair and rock while he talks, or lean back against the pillows. Ask him what he can do when he feels like that, instead of hitting, kicking, and yelling. He likes to paint. Can he paint up a storm? If he agrees, you can set up a private painting spot for him: an easel or flat painting on a table away from the others, or finger painting on a table or the floor. Ask him to show you the painting afterward and tell you what it feels like. When he feels like that again, can he come to you and have you help him get started on another painting? Can he put his feelings into a painting where they won't hurt anybody? (See Figure 21–1.)

FIGURE 21–1 The Child Crayoned a Dark Hole and Put His Feelings in It.

6. Talk with the other children involved.

- Later go to the other boys who teased Andre and ask them how they think Andre felt. Not whose fault it was, but how did Andre feel? What would make anyone feel like that? Would they like to feel like that? Children often pick on other youngsters whom they know will lose their tempers and get into trouble. Remind these youngsters that theirs is a caring community where they all need to care for one another. Can they be caring toward Andre? How? Can they help Andre be caring toward them? How?

REFERENCES AND SUGGESTED READINGS

Beaty, J. J. (1999). *Prosocial guidance for the preschool child.* Upper Saddle River, NJ: Merrill/Prentice Hall.

Beaty, J. J. (2004). *Skills for preschool teachers* (7th ed.). Upper Saddle River, NJ: Merrill/Prentice Hall.

Greenspan, S. I. (1997). *The growth of the mind and the endangered origins of intelligence.* Reading, MA: Addison-Wesley.

Morrison, K. L. (2004). Positive adult/child interactions: Strategies that support children's healthy development. *Dimensions, 32*(2), 23–28.

Stone, J. (1993). Caregiver and teacher language—Responsive or restrictive? *Young Children, 48*(4), 12–18.

22 JEALOUSY

CONCEPT

"He always gets the biggest piece!" "She always gets to be leader!" "You always serve him first!" "He always gets to choose the best toys!" Have you heard anything like this from your children lately? Both at home and in the early childhood classroom you are listening to the complaints of *jealousy:* that someone is better, nicer, more privileged, or better liked than the complainer.

Jealousy is an emotional state that seems to be inherent in the human race. At some time or other almost everyone feels its pangs: sibling rivalry at home, professional jealousy in the workplace, or relationship jealousies between men and women. Is there some way we can dampen its destructiveness in the early childhood classroom to prevent its appearance later in life? Can't children learn how to deal with it if they understand what it is about?

Unfortunately when anyone—child or adult—is caught in its throes, it is difficult to extricate themselves. Early childhood teachers can, however, bring jealousy to the attention of the children in ways that may help them deal with it vicariously. By hearing stories read to them about characters experiencing jealous feelings, they can think about it rationally and decide what they would do in similar situations. Ramsey (1991) points out:

> Reading stories about characters who have the same kinds of feelings in similar situations helps young children begin to understand their own emotions and why they must change them. Children's books are a primary vehicle for this kind of teaching. By engaging children in stories, we enable our young readers and listeners to empathize with different points of view and experience a wide range of social dilemmas. (p. 91)

STEPS

1. **Read simple books with characters children can identify with who have jealousy problems.**
2. **Reread one book several times until the children are familiar with it.**
3. **Ask children to choose what character they would like to be for a story reenactment.**
4. **You become the narrator who reads the story while the actors play their roles.**
5. **Perform the drama for the class with new actors as many times as the children want.**

ACTIVITIES

1. **Read simple books with characters children can identify with who have jealousy problems.**
   - *I Love You the Purplest* (from the list in Figure 22–1) is a story about a mother and her two boys, Max and Julian, who pester her constantly to tell them who is the best. The wise mother gives them answers that satisfy them and don't let them feel jealousy toward one another. For example: Who has the best worms for fishing? Mother tells them Max has the liveliest and Julian has the juiciest. Who is the best boat rower? Mother tells them Julian takes the deepest strokes and Max's strokes are fastest. At bedtime they ask who do you love best? Mother says she loves Julian the bluest, Max the reddest, and both together the purplest.

FIGURE 22–1   Books with
Jealousy Themes.

> *I Love You the Purplest* (Joose, 1996)
>
> *I Want One Too!* (Ehrmantraat, 2003)*
>
> *Noisy Nora* (Wells, 1997)
>
> *Pet Show* (Keats, 1972)*
>
> *Peter's Chair* (Keats, 1967)*
>
> *Barfburger Baby, I Was Here First* (Danziger, 2004)

*multicultural

- *I Want One Too!* is not so much a jealousy story as the tale of little Megan who is 3 and would be jealous if she didn't get exactly the same thing as her brother William who is 6: ice cream, sliding down a slide, sitting side by side, eating a snack. William finally plays a not-so-nice trick on her to get her to stop when he has to go to the doctor's to get a shot and Megan wants one, too.

- *Noisy Nora,* the attention-getter in chapter 3, shows jealousy of her little brother and sister because her parents are always doing things with them and not Nora. So Nora creates a huge fuss by banging a window, slamming a door, and spilling her sister's marbles on the floor. Finally, as a last desperate measure she runs away.

- *Pet Show* has all the neighborhood children bringing their pets to the show to see whose is best. All the children get prize ribbons for their pets: the noisiest parrot, the handsomest frog, the yellowest canary, the busiest ant, the longest dog. But Archie can't find his cat so he brings an empty jar to the show with his pet in it: a germ. The judges give it a prize for being the quietest pet! Do your children understand that the judges prevented any jealousy and hard feelings by giving the same prize ribbons to everyone for the special feature of their pet?

- *Peter's Chair* tells the story of Peter who is jealous of his new baby sister. When he sees his father painting his old crib and highchair pink, he knows his little blue chair will be next. So he takes the chair and runs away. But he is too big to fit in it anymore, so he returns and offers to paint it with his father.

2. **Reread one book several times until the children are familiar with it.**
   - In one class the children liked *Peter's Chair* very much because they also had problems adjusting to a new baby. The teacher read it several times until the children knew it well. Just reading a story to young children does not mean they truly understand what it is about. But stories they really enjoy and want you to read again and again are the ones they come to understand if they can take on the roles of the characters.

3. **Ask children to choose what character they would like to be for a story reenactment.**
   - Have them choose to be one of the characters in *Peter's Chair:* mother, father, and Peter. Some of the children wanted to play the part of the baby, although she doesn't appear in the book. Fine. The characters do not need to wear costumes for their roles unless they want to. (The baby character wore a bib.) They can make name tags or head bands to wear. Talk to them about how they think their character should act, but let them play the roles any way they want.

4. **You become the narrator who reads the story while the actors play their roles.**
   - Story reenactments are impromptu dramas for the children only. The audience can be the other children in the class. The characters can make up their lines, say the lines in the book as you read them, or just do the actions with no dialog. You can repeat the reenactments as many times as you have children who want to be characters. Don't forget to have the audience clap after each performance.

5. **Perform the drama for the class with new actors as many times as the children want.**
   - Repetition is important for young children's learning. It is not necessary to have new actors every time. Once everyone who wants one has had a turn, let the original actors repeat their roles. As Ishee and Goldhaber (1990) tell us:

Children can make paper hats, head bands, or masks for their roles.

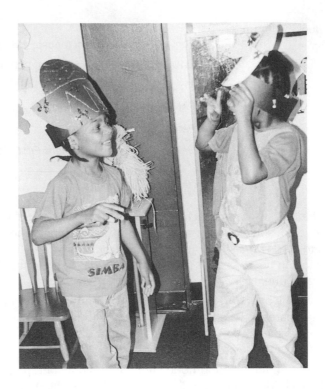

This is the most important part. Many repetitions help children. For many children it is necessary to watch a play numerous times before making that first gesture of pretense within the play. For others, repetition allows an opportunity to elaborate and expand on the story as presented, to take on a variety of roles, and to assume major responsibility for a role. (p. 74)

They tell how one of their classes performed *The Three Bears* 27 times in four days!

- Another way to reenact stories is to use puppets for the characters. You don't need a puppet stage but only the hand puppets themselves for the children to act out their roles as you read the story. Not only do children begin to understand the concept of jealousy through these reenactments, but their early reading skills get a tremendous boost.

REFERENCES AND SUGGESTED READINGS

Beaty, J. J. (1995). *Converting conflicts in preschool programs.* Clifton Park, NY: Thomson Delmar Learning.

Greenspan, S. (1999). *Building healthy minds.* New York: Perseus Book Group.

Ishee, N., & Goldhaber, J. (1990). Story re-enactment: Let the play begin! *Young Children, 45*(3), 70–75.

Ramsey, P. G. (1991). *Making friends in school: Promoting peer relationships in early childhood.* New York: Teachers College Press.

Children's Books

Danziger, P. (2004). *Barfburger Baby, I was here first.* New York: Putnam's Sons.

Ehrmantraat, B. (2003). *I want one too!* Jamestown, ND: Bubble Gum Press.*

Joose, B. M. (1996). *I love you the purplest.* San Francisco: Chronicle Books.

Keats, E. J. (1967). *Peter's chair.* New York: Puffin Books.*

Keats, E. J. (1972). *Pet show.* New York: Puffin Books.*

Wells, R. (1997). *Noisy Nora.* New York: Dial Books.

_____

*multicultural

23 LIMITS

CONCEPT

All young children need limits: the lively 4-year-olds who come bounding into the classroom daily full of explosive energy, the know-it-all 5's ready to impose their wills on everyone, and even the shy 3's soon to be as vivacious as the rest. All of them expect the teachers to keep their exuberance within limits, to prevent them from getting hurt or hurting others, and to keep the classroom running smoothly. What they don't realize at first is it is not you alone who will keep them within limits, but they themselves. As Brazelton and Sparrow (2001) tell us:

> *Limits are reliable expectations. They provide a safe foundation on which children can begin to discover that they can stop themselves when they feel out of control.* (p. 307)

How limits and rules are formed is discussed in more detail in chapter 37: Rule-making. Here we look at the need for limits and how limits are applied. Limits are needed in early childhood classrooms for protection of the children, the adults, and the materials in the room (Hearron & Hildebrand, 2005). They are also needed to teach children positive behavior in group situations.

Limits should be clear to understand, simple to express, and few in number. In this caring community of yours, children must learn not to hurt one another, themselves, or the materials—three easily understood and simple rules that everyone can learn to abide by.

We do not hurt others.

We do not hurt ourselves

We do not hurt our materials.

Some teachers object to using negative words such as "not hurt." They would rather state limits in positive terms. As Hearron and Hildebrand (2005) tell us:

Be safe.

Be kind to others.

Take care of our room. (p. 312)

If this works better for you and if your children understand them clearly, these are limits you can use. How do children learn about limits?

STEPS

1. **Staff members must all agree on limits and how to apply them in a consistent, firm, but not harsh manner.**
2. **When you notice a child following the limits, you should point it out.**
3. **When you notice a child not following the limits, you must intervene and tell the child what is not allowed.**

ACTIVITIES

1. **Staff members must all agree on limits and how to apply them in a consistent, firm, but not harsh manner.**

   • Limits should be discussed and agreed upon at a preservice meeting of all staff members so there is no misunderstanding of what they are: brief, simple, and few in number; and how they must be applied by everyone: consistently, firmly, but not harshly. Substitutes, volunteers, and student interns should also be briefed about the limits you follow and what their roles are.

   • Staff members need to be made aware that these limits are for protecting children and helping them to know what behavior is allowed and what is not allowed.

   • Everyone should learn to help children follow the limits in a positive way that respects them as people, but may require them to stop or change their behavior. As Hyson (2004) warns: "Young children also need to be sure that teachers will not reject or abandon them if they violate classroom rules" (p. 46).

2. **When you notice a child following the limits, you should point it out.**

   • It is not necessary to make a fuss about limits. Simply inform individuals when they follow them as well as when they don't. When a teacher notices a child following the limits, she can point it out. "Richie, you remembered about being safe. Thanks for giving Clayton your pair of safety goggles to wear at the sand table." Or, "Makaila, thanks for telling Amber to say it in words and not hit Cassy for taking her crayons. That's helping her be kind."

   • If following limits is difficult for a number of the children, especially at the beginning of the year, you may want to make a sticker chart with the three limits stated earlier. Children can print their initials on a sticker and put it on the chart when they have followed a limit. If teachers notice there are few stickers for being kind or taking care of the room, they can talk about it to a small group at a time. How can the children be kind to one another, for instance? What should they be doing to take care of the room? Then be sure to notice and thank children who have followed these limits.

3. **When you notice a child not following the limits, you must intervene and tell the child what is not allowed.**

   • Hitting, pushing, pinching, and even teasing another child hurts. When this happens, a teacher should intervene quickly to stop it, at the same time telling the child what is not allowed. This should happen every time a child oversteps the bounds.

   • Once certain children understand which classroom limits they are not following, they need to learn ways to keep themselves within the bounds. Shouldn't they be punished for continually hitting other children or destroying materials, you may ask? Some kind of consequence must occur, but it should be directed toward helping them change their behavior, not making them stop their behavior for fear of punishment.

   • One teacher invented "puppet time." Puppet time was the time when the Oh-Oh Puppet came out to talk and listen privately to the child. A child who had overstepped the rules had to tell the puppet what he had done, and how he was going to remember not to do that again. Sometimes the teacher wore the puppet on her hand to talk and listen to the child. But often the child would take the puppet to a private space and talk to it. When he was finished he needed to come back to the teacher and tell her what he had decided. She would then write it down in a notebook so she could keep track of what the child decided to do. One child wanted to wear the Oh-Oh Puppet on his hand for a whole morning to remind him not to hit. The teacher agreed—and it worked.

This teacher talks to a boy about how he can remember to be kind and not take things from another child without asking.

REFERENCES AND SUGGESTED READINGS

Brazelton, T. B., & Sparrow, J. D. (2001). *Touchpoints three to six: Your child's emotional and behavioral development.* Cambridge, MA: Perseus Publishing.

Greenspan, S. (1999). *Building healthy minds.* New York: Da Capo Press.

Hearron, P. F., & Hildebrand, V. (2005). *Guiding young children.* Upper Saddle River, NJ: Merrill/Prentice Hall.

Hyson, M. (2004). *The emotional development of young children: Building an emotion-centered curriculum* (2nd ed.). New York: Teachers College Press.

24

MATERIALS, CALMING

CONCEPT

When young children experience an emotional upheaval, positive guidance offers several ways to help them release stressful feelings and become calm again. They can sit and rock by themselves or with a staff member, retreat to one of the private spaces described in chapter 12: Environment, throw bean-bags at a target, bounce on an individual trampoline, listen to music with headsets, or become involved in one of the calming materials described here.

Water, play dough, sand, finger paints, scissors and paper scraps, book tapes, puppets or character dolls, and soft objects such as pillows or stuffed animals can be used to calm distressed or out-of-control children. Such materials should be kept apart from the regular classroom activities in a special location for children to select and use by themselves or with a teacher's help during difficult times.

STEPS

1. **Set up a private tub of water with pouring and squeezing toys.**
2. **Have a private table or tray for finger painting.**
3. **Have a private container of sand with little figures of people, animals, and vehicles.**
4. **Use book tapes, character dolls, or puppets in a private pillow-filled nook.**

ACTIVITIES

1. **Set up a private tub of water with pouring and squeezing toys.**
   - Water play has always been a popular activity in early childhood programs. Children love the feel of it and the way they can splash it, pour it, or squirt it. As a therapeutic material water can help a distressed child to squeeze away his feelings with sponges of different sizes or a baster, or by filling plastic bottles and pouring them out, or by turning an egg beater to make bubbles, or simply by swishing his hands around in it. As Crosser (1994) notes:

     Water is intriguing. It seems to draw children to explore its structure and properties. The thoughtful teacher can structure the environment and materials to make the most of water play. (p. 28)

2. **Have a private table or tray for finger painting.**
   - Finger painting has long been used to soothe upset children and help them to release unwanted feelings, possibly because swishing paint with the hands has the same mesmerizing effect that water does. Place a gob of paint on butcher paper, a tabletop, or a tray and have children move it around with one hand or two while making a myriad of swirls, designs, or handprints—and then wipe them away with one swish. If they wish to preserve some of their designs they can press absorbent paper on them and rub. Cherry (1972), in her classic book, *Creative Art for the Developing Child,* has this to say:

     The rhythmic movement and sensory experience provide avenues for the free expression of feelings and healthy emotional release, and the good feelings that accompany fingerpainting open the way to increased social growth. (p. 105)

Water play can help a distressed child become calm again.

3. **Have a private container of sand with little figures of people, animals, and vehicles.**

    *   A private sand table can be set up in a small tub just as you did with water. Children enjoy the feel of sifting their fingers through sand and pouring it out of containers just like water. In addition they can role play with the little figures of people, animals, and vehicles you provide, creating their own world. Sand can also be made available for children's relaxation on a tray rather than in a tub. Always be sure children wear safety goggles when playing with sand. Wheat (1995) has found:

        > *The very process of working with the sand tray regularly has helped some children immensely. Teachers have discussed how they have watched children work through sadness, anger, and disappointment and finally return to the group in a relaxed state. (p. 82)*

4. **Use book tapes, character dolls, or puppets in a private pillow-filled nook.**

    *   Children's books are best read to the youngsters in your class by a live person, but for children who need to get away by themselves to cool down and relax, you can provide some of the books discussed in this text along with a tape cassette. The child can be located in a cozy corner filled with pillows where he or she listens to one of the books using a headset while she turns the pages of the book when the signal is given. Some of these books also have character dolls that children can play with afterward.

    *   Paperback and hardcover books that come with cassettes from Weston Woods (1-800-243-5020) include the following:

    Paperback

    Pet Show (Keats, 1972)

    Peter's Chair (Keats, 1967)

    Whistle for Willie (Keats, 1964)

    Blueberries for Sal (McCloskey, 1948)

    Noisy Nora (Wells, 1997)

Children can play with paper doll book characters as if they are real.

Too Many Tamales (Soto, 1993)

Where the Wild Things Are (Sendak, 1963)

Hardcover

Amazing Grace (Hoffman, 1991)

Click, Clack, Moo Cows that Type (Cronin, 2000)

How Do Dinosaurs Say Goodnight? (Yolen, 2000)

- The following character dolls for some of these books can be ordered from Demco (1-800-356-1200):

Grace doll from *Amazing Grace*

Wild things puppets from *Where the Wild Things Are*

Peter doll from *Whistle for Willie*

- For books with no dolls or puppets available you can cut out and laminate the characters from an extra paperback copy or the dust jacket of a hardcover book. Children enjoy playing with and making up adventures for these paper dolls just as if they were real. As Warash (2004) tells us:

> *Paper dolls, like other age-old toys, are simple and allow room for imaginative growth. Children can use the dolls to re-enact scenarios that enable them to grasp day-to-day circumstances. Through doll play, children often resolve delicate and complex issues that they have on their minds. (p. 10)*

REFERENCES AND SUGGESTED READINGS

Beaty, J. J. (1999). *Prosocial guidance for the preschool child.* Upper Saddle River, NJ: Merrill/Prentice Hall.

Cherry, C. (1972). *Creative art for the developing child.* Belmont, CA: Fearon Publishers.

Crosser, S. (1994). Making the most of water play. *Young Children, 49*(5), 28–32.

Warash, B. G. (2004). Paper dolls: Back to basics with a contemporary twist. *Dimensions of Early Childhood, 32*(1), 10–15.

Wheat, R. (1995). Help children work through emotional difficulties—Sand trays are great! *Young Children, 51*(1), 82–83.

Children's Books

Cronin, D. (2000). *Click, clack, moo cows that type.* New York: Simon & Schuster.

Hoffman, M. (1991). *Amazing Grace.* New York: Dial Books.*

Keats, E. J. (1964). *Whistle for Willie.* New York: Viking Press.*

Keats, E. J. (1967). *Peter's chair.* New York: Puffin Books.*

Keats, E. J. (1972). *Pet show.* New York: Puffin Books.*

McCloskey, R. (1948). *Blueberries for Sal.* New York: Viking Press.

Sendak, M. (1963). *Where the wild things are.* New York: HarperCollins.

Soto, G. (1993). *Too many tamales.* New York: Penguin Putnam.*

Wells, R. (1997). *Noisy Nora.* New York: Dial Books.

Yolen, J. (2000). *How do dinosaurs say good night?* New York: Blue Sky Press.*

———————

*multicultural

25 MOODS

CONCEPT

Do young children experience moods like older children and adults? Of course, they do. Moods are emotional states that show on children's faces and in their actions how they are feeling. They can be sad, glad, angry, happy, excited—the whole gamut of emotions that everyone experiences. But when we speak of a child being moody, we usually mean she is being uncommunicative and withdrawn, often sad or dispirited. Such moodiness can be the result of a loss of some kind: a person leaving, a pet missing, a treasured possession lost, or sometimes because a friend won't speak to her.

Some moods come over children for reasons even they don't understand. They may have heard something at home that makes them uneasy, or someone has acted toward them in an unpleasant manner. Some children are more moody than others because of their particular temperament. As McDevitt and Ormrod (2004) note:

> Many aspects of temperament, such as cheerfulness, outgoingness, moodiness, and anxiety, probably have a genetic basis. Yet the genetic basis for temperament is best thought of as only a predisposition to behave in a certain way. (pp. 379–380)

Such a predisposition can be modified by experience. If you note that a certain child is acting moody, you may be able to help him feel better through the personal activities you involve him in. Adults talk about feeling "blue" when they feel bad. Using certain colors has been shown to affect children's moods, too (Cherry, 1972, p. 34).

Taylor (2002) tells about color in classroom learning centers influencing even academic achievement.

> Red is a good choice for areas planned for gross motor activities and concept development activities; yellow is good for music and art activities; and green, blue, and purple are effective in reading areas. (p. 369)

STEPS

1. **Read a book with a moodiness or color theme on a one-to-one basis.**
2. **Engage the child in an art activity involving colors.**
3. **Engage the child in a music/movement activity involving colors.**

ACTIVITIES

1. **Read a book with a moodiness or color theme on a one-to-one basis.**
   - Reading a book with a moodiness theme does not always work. It depends on the child and his temperament. If he will talk to you about what is bothering him, you can then decide if reading a book will help, as well as which book you should read. Figure 25–1 offers some good choices.

FIGURE 25–1 Books with
Moodiness or Color Themes.

> *Maisy's Rainbow Dream* (Cousins, 2003)
>
> *Yesterday I Had the Blues* (Frame, 2003)
>
> *Kinda Blue* (Grifalconi, 1993)
>
> *My Crayons Talk* (Hubbard, 1996)
>
> *Color Dance* (Jonas, 1989)
>
> *Red Day Green Day* (Kunhardt, 1992)
>
> *The Bad Mood* (Petz, 2004)

- You may want to start by reading *Yesterday I Had the Blues,* about the African American city family with the boy narrator who yesterday had "those deep down in my shoes blues." But today he has the greens that make you want to be somebody. His daddy has the grays, his sister has the pinks, Gran's got the yellows, and Mama's got the reds: look out! But together they have a family, and that's golden. Does your listener identify with any of the characters or colors? Can he tell you what it feels like to have the blues or the reds? Can he draw a picture showing what he feels like? Put out all of your color markers.

2. **Engage the child in an art activity involving colors.**

   - Read *Maisy's Rainbow Dream* to a child who needs cheering up as a lead-in to an art activity. Every page is a different color in this large rainbow-hued book. As Maisy the mouse sleeps on one page, she visualizes all sorts of fantastic objects on the opposite page: a tee-shirted alligator flying with a red polka-dot umbrella, a blue-and-white teapot and cup walking away, a watermelon-slice turtle with a pineapple on its head. Can the child close her eyes and look for her own rainbow dream? Put out crayons or markers if she tells you about something she saw with her eyes closed. One girl drew and captioned the picture in Figure 25–2.

Talk with the moody child to see what is bothering him and whether reading a book or coloring a picture would help.

FIGURE 25–2 It's a
Rainbow Potato That
Escaped with Legs.

3. **Engage the child in a music/movement activity involving colors.**

   • Read *Color Dance* as a lead-in to a music and movement activity if this seems appropriate. Some children just need to get out of themselves to break their moodiness. *Color Dance* shows three children in red, yellow, and blue leotards carrying filmy scarves of the same colors. As they dance a light shines through the scarves, mixing the colors and creating new ones: red and yellow make orange, yellow and blue make green, red and blue make purple. Mix them all together and they make browns and grays.

   • Can your child do a color dance with two other children? Transparent fabric scarves in red, yellow, and blue can be purchased from fabric shops or from Lakeshore Learning Materials (1-800-778-4456) along with the book and cassette *Musical Scarves Activities*. Ask the children how the colors make them feel. Have them change scarves and dance again. Do their feelings change?

REFERENCES AND SUGGESTED READINGS

Cherry, C. (1972). *Creative art for the developing child.* Belmont, CA: Fearon.

Curtis, D., & Carter, M. (2003). *Designs for living and learning: Transforming early childhood environments.* St. Paul, MN: Redleaf Press.

Lazenby, G. (2000). *The healing home.* Guilford, CT: The Lyons Press.

McDevitt, T. M., & Ormrod, J. E. (2004). *Child development: Educating and working with children and adolescents.* Upper Saddle River, NJ: Merrill/Prentice Hall.

Taylor, B. J. (2002). *Early childhood program management: People and procedures.* Upper Saddle River, NJ: Merrill/Prentice Hall.

Children's Books

Cousins, L. (2003). *Maisy's rainbow dream.* Cambridge, MA: Candlewick Press.

Frame, J. A. (2003). *Yesterday I had the blues.* Berkeley, CA: Tricycle Press.*

Grifalconi, A. (1993). *Kinda blue.* Boston: Little, Brown.*

Hubbard, P. (1996). *My crayons talk.* New York: Henry Holt.

Jonas, A. (1989). *Color dance.* New York: Greenwillow Books.*

Kunhardt, E. (1992). *Red day green day.* New York: Greenwillow Books.

Petz, M. (2004). *The bad mood.* New York: North-South Books.

*multicultural

26 MOVEMENT

CONCEPT

Movement is always helpful when change is necessary. So long as it doesn't get out of hand, spontaneous movement can help young children overcome upsetting feelings and get back on the right track again. Children already use movement to express their feelings. See them wiggle and squirm with impatience when they have to wait too long for something to happen, jump up and down when they are excited about something, and rush to get in line when it's time to go out.

Do you as a teacher spend too much time waiting for the children to settle down and return to "normal"? Spontaneous movement is normal for young children and can be a dynamic learning tool for the creative teacher.

As adults, many of us have lost much of our early spontaneity. Yet when we stop to reflect, we realize that we often do express feelings through movement. Even something as simple as walking can express our mood if we: stomp, clomp, tramp, stamp, or tread heavily; or if we trudge, shuffle, hobble, shamble, or scuffle morosely. Children do the same. Watch and see.

Activities that express emotions through basic movements such as walking, running, jumping, leaping, and hopping can help children release unwanted feelings if used appropriately. Group movements can also free individuals of emotions pent up inside them. How do children walk when they feel happy? How do they walk when they feel sad? Have volunteers demonstrate. You can tap out a rhythm on a drum or clap your hands to get them started. Or you can demonstrate how you would walk. Can the children tell by your movements how you feel?

Some children may be just too shy to try moving on their own. They may need some kind of prop to hide behind or a book character to do the moving for them. Animals are great movers. Do children know how rabbits hop through a garden? How deer bound through the woods? What about a kangaroo? A mouse? A snake?

STEPS

1. **Have colored scarves, capes, and ribbons on sticks as props for children to move to music.**

2. **Have pictures of animals on cards or posters for children to choose and move as the animal moves.**

3. **Have a "movement ring" (hula hoop) on the floor and have one child at a time demonstrate movements to express words.**

4. **Read books about animals who move, and put out stuffed animals that a child can move like the animal book character.**

ACTIVITIES

1. **Have colored scarves, capes, and ribbons on sticks as props for children to move to music.**

   • Have children choose a prop to move with. Ask a child to demonstrate how each prop works by waving a scarf around, running with a cape over the shoulders, or twirling a long ribbon on a stick in huge circles. If shy children concentrate on moving a prop, they may find themselves moving without embarrassment. Put on a record, tape, or CD with peppy instrumental music, and have children run around while moving their props. Lakeshore (1-800-778-4456) offers the following movement CDs and cassettes:

Big Fun	*Five Little Monkeys*
Dance Party Fun	*Beanbag Rock & Roll*
Wiggle Wiggle	*Kids in Action*
Jump-Start Action Songs	*The Wiggles Yummy Yummy*

2. **Have pictures of animals on cards or posters for children to choose and move as the animal moves.**

   • Children can choose a card, turn it over so no one can see the animal, and then move like the animal. Can anyone guess what animal it is? Accept any movement the child makes. Lakeshore has an animal photo library with 170 cards with animal photos, as well as a science poster series with 60 different animals and where they live.

3. **Have a "movement ring" (hula hoop) on the floor and have one child at a time demonstrate movements to express words.**

   • Work with one small group at a time. First have them watch while volunteers show different kinds of movements within the ring: hopping on one foot, jumping up and down, running in place, marching in place, bending, swaying, turning round and round, making upper body go round and round, twirling, or galloping in place. Swing arms back and forth. Swim with arms. Bend and touch toes. Twirl. Climb in place with arms and feet. Can children think of any other movements?

   • Talk to the children about using movements to communicate feeling words. Have different children demonstrate with movements inside the circle the following words:

"Help me, I'm falling!"	"Watch out!"	"I won!"
"Oh, I'm lost!"	"I'm so tired!"	"I feel terrible!"
"Stop hitting me!"	"I'm scared!"	"I'm mad at you!"

   Can young children do pantomime like this? Try it and see. Accept any movements they make. Let different children try the same words. What words of their own would they like to demonstrate? How do they feel afterward?

It's easy to move like a bear if you're wearing a bear costume.

4. **Read books about animals who move, and put out stuffed animals that a child can move like the animal book character.**

- Read *Giraffes Can't Dance* (Andreae, 2001) and ask someone to choose the stuffed giraffe and try to follow Gerald's movements: first stumbling and then really dancing.
- Read *Dinosaurumpus* (Mitton, 2002) and have children choose to move the various dinosaurs you have put out for them like their motions in the story.
- Read *Hop Jump* (Walsh, 1993) and put three hula hoops down on the floor to represent lily pads. Have a "Lily Pad Leap" with the different children being frogs that leap from one hoop to another like the frogs in the story. Have the child that is Betsy stop in each hoop and twirl around (dance). Then one-by-one have the other children stop and twirl until there is only one child left that would rather leap than dance.
- Two more excellent books about animals that move are *Down by the Cool of the Pool* (Mitton, 2001) and *Hilda Must Be Dancing* (Wilson, 2004).

Most children enjoy playing the Lily Pad Leap game more than any other movement game. If this is true with your children, think of other similar movement games that express emotions they could play by jumping into the hoops on the floor. (If you don't have hoops, make circles from contact paper or circle outlines with masking tape.) As Hannaford (1995) tells us:

> *Children who are allowed to naturally and responsibly express emotions are better able to constructively or creatively use them throughout life.* (p. 59)

REFERENCES AND SUGGESTED READINGS

Beaty, J. J. (1995). *Converting conflicts in preschool.* Clifton Park, NY: Thomson Delmar Learning.

Chenfield, M. B. (2004). Education is a moving experience. Get Movin'! *Young Children 59*(4), 56–58.

Hannaford, C. (1995). *Smart moves: Why learning is not all in your head.* Arlington, VA: Great Ocean Publishing.

Sanders, S. W. (1992). *Designing preschool movement programs.* Champaign, IL: Human Kinetics.

Sanders, S. W. (2002). *Active for life: Developmentally appropriate movement programs for young children.* Washington, DC: National Association for the Education of Young Children.

Children's Books

Andreae, G. (2001). *Giraffes can't dance.* New York: Orchard Books.

Mitton, T. (2001). *Down by the cool of the pool.* New York: Orchard Books.

Mitton, T. (2002). *Dinosaurumpus.* New York: Orchard Books.

Walsh, E. S. (1993). *Hop jump.* San Diego: Harcourt Brace.

Wilson, K. (2004). *Hilda must be dancing.* New York: Margaret K. McElderry Books.

27 MUSIC

CONCEPT

Music soothes the wild beast, so they say. Can it also soothe the wild child? It can, and so much more. Until recent brain research turned up the amazing power of music, most early childhood practitioners had no idea of the real importance of music in the young child's classroom. Neuroscientist Frank Wilson (1986), who registered brain scans of children as they performed similar tasks, reports that when children read words the language centers of their brain light up on his scanner; but when they read music the entire brain "lights up like a Christmas tree."

Music seems to synchronize the two hemispheres of the brain by stimulating emotions, which then focus a person's attention and heighten motivation. Electro-encephalogram tests show that music actually alters brain waves, making the brain more receptive to learning (Davies, 2000, p. 148). According to Campbell (1992), "music rhythmically and harmonically stimulates essential patterns of brain growth" (p. 53).

When does such growth occur? The critical period for the development of the brain's "music center" takes place during the preschool and early elementary years. Exposure to music during these years is essential for this brain development. According to Snyder (1997):

> Music and other arts that evoke emotional response appear to open the gate to the neurocortex and higher level thinking. Music stimulates and motivates critical thinking. (p. 166)

What does this mean to early childhood teachers? First of all, it means we should fill the environment with music. Not loud record playing but personal uses of song. For example, singing directions instead of saying them; singing greetings; or singing or chanting simple nursery rhymes to help children notice things like weather, food, clothes, and feelings can encourage children to express their own feelings and actions in song by copying yours. Can children really learn to do this? They can if you are the model.

Put aside your fears of not being able to sing in front of others, of not being able to carry a tune. Of course you can do it. Start with simple chanting. Say a chant first and then sing it in a monotone. Have children repeat your chants the same way until they know them by heart. Find picture books that illustrate simple chants and songs and read/sing them together. How does it make you feel? What about the children?

Because music so strongly affects emotions, it can be very useful in helping young children control their own powerful emotions. Just as lullabies help make young children drowsy, humming can help calm upset children, as well. Lazy tunes hummed in a slow, repetitive beat can soothe ruffled feathers, while peppy tunes hummed in a lively tempo can brighten bruised feelings. Put your own words to the tunes and your message will get across to the children better than any plain talk can do.

Teachers and children need to hum together, chant together, and sing together. Using a record or CD can also be useful in stressful situations if it involves some kind of interaction (singing, moving, or playing an instrument) and if it is done together. Child development expert and banjo player Jim Gill (1998) points out: "Music helps establish a comfortable feeling in the learning environment by allowing the teacher to share something with the kids" (p. 36). What can you share musically?

STEPS

1. **Sing rather than say directions.**
2. **Chant/sing nursery rhymes and jump rope rhymes, using your own words.**
3. **Read/sing song picture books together.**

ACTIVITIES

1. **Sing rather than say directions.**
   - Do children pay attention when you give them a direction? ("It's time to pick the blocks up, boys.") They will, if you *sing* the directions. Consider the different directions you say in words every day, and how you can convert each one to a simple song. For example:

   It's clean-up time.

   Time to go outside.

   Get ready for lunch.

   Everybody clean off your table.

   Everybody brush your teeth.

   Time to get ready for nap.

   Get out your cots for nap.

   - Not only will the children listen to your singing directions, they will feel so much better about following them. Songs make everyone feel good. Try using some of the familiar tunes from the traditional nursery songs in Figure 27–1 for your directions.

   Clean-up directions

   Hickory dickory dock,   Put the clothes back on the hooks,

   It's time to pick up blocks,   On the hooks, on the hooks,

   It's time for Samantha   Put the dishes on the shelves

   And also Brianna,   It's time to go outside.

   It's time to pick up blocks.   (Tune: *London Bridge*)

   (Tune: *Hickory Dickory Dock*)

FIGURE 27–1 Traditional Nursery Songs.

Alphabet Song	Jack and Jill
Are You Sleeping?	John Jacob Jingleheimer Schmidt
Do the Hokey Pokey	London Bridge Is Falling Down
Down By the Station	Mary Had a Little Lamb
Eentsy Weentsy Spider	Ring Around the Rosy
Go In & Out the Windows	Row, Row, Row Your Boat
Here We Go Looby Loo	Shoo Fly
Here We Go Round	Three Blind Mice
Hickory Dickory Dock	Twinkle, Twinkle Little Star
If You're Happy	Wheels on the Bus
I'm a Little Teapot	Where Is Thumbkin?

Get Ready for Lunch

Are you hungry? Are you hungry?   Go find yourself a partner,
Line up here; wash your hands;   Go find yourself a partner,
Time to put the plates down,   Go find yourself a partner,
Time to put the napkins down,   And sit right down to eat.
Sit right down; time to eat.   (Tune: *Go in and out the Windows*)
(Tune: *Are You Sleeping?*)

2. **Chant/sing nursery rhymes and jump rope rhymes, using your own words.**

    • If you notice some weather condition you want the children to notice, sing or chant a little song about it.

Wind

Blow, blow, blow so hard,   If it's blowing and it's snowing,
We will stay inside,   Clap your hands!
Jennifer, Jessica, Stephanie too,   If it's blowing and it's snowing,
We will stay inside.   Stamp your feet!
(Tune: *Row, Row, Row Your Boat*)   If it's blowing and it's snowing,
                                             And there's no place we are going,
                                             We will just sit down right here
                                             And we will eat!
                                             (Tune: *If You're Happy and You Know It*)

3. **Read/sing song picture books together.**

    • Song picture books (also called sing-along stories) have become very popular with teachers because of their use in teaching reading. Children can predict what words will come next because they already know the songs. Be sure to read familiar book songs to one small group at a time, so they can see the pictures that illustrate the words. After the first reading it's time to sing the book song together. Go slow at first and turn the pages as children sing the words. If children really like the book and song, some may want to reenact the story as you sing, or to stand up and do body action motions or finger plays. Some song picture books that children enjoy are provided in Figure 27–2.

    • In *Skip to My Lou* a farmer boy and his dog wait until the farmer and his wife have gone out for the day, and then they begin the riotous "skip to my Lou" with cats in the buttermilk, pigs in the parlor, cows in the kitchen, and sheep in the bathtub. As you read or the group sings the words, children who have chosen to be the various animals can act out their parts or sing

FIGURE 27–2 Song Picture Books.

There Was a Bold Lady Who Wanted a Star (Harper, 2002)

Miss Mary Mack (Hoberman, 1998)

Mary Had a Little Lamb (Hoberman, 2003)

The Seals on the Bus (Hort, 2000)

The Wheels on the Bus (Kowalski, 1987)

I Know an Old Lady Who Swallowed a Pie (Jackson, 1997)

There Was an Old Lady Who Swallowed a Trout! (Sloat, 1998)

The Itsy Bitsy Spider (Trapani, 1988)

I Know an Old Lady Who Swallowed a Fly (Westcott, 1980)

Skip to My Lou (Westcott, 1989)

The Lady with the Alligator Purse (Westcott, 1988)

Some children may want to stand up and act out the parts while singing the song.

their words. Everyone can clap for the chorus, and then scramble to get the house picked up before the farmer and his wife return. Make repeat performances go faster and faster until everyone collapses in laughter.

- Some song books lend themselves to finger plays (*Itsy Bitsy Spider*) or body action movements (the old woman swallowing things), or making loud noises (*The Seals on the Bus*). In *Miss Mary Mack* you may want to speed up repeating the words three times (Mack, Mack, Mack, etc.) until children once again collapse in laughter.

- As you can see, song picture books bring both music and laughter into the classroom, brightening everyone's spirits. Giles (1991) believes that "the right music at the right time can make [children] less stressed, more relaxed, happier, and more productive" (p. 44).

REFERENCES AND SUGGESTED READINGS

Campbell, D. G. (1992). *100 ways to improve teaching using your voice and music.* Tucson, AZ: Zephyr Press.

Davies, M. A. (2000). Learning . . . The beat goes on. *Childhood Education, 76*(3), 148–153.

Giles, M. M. (1991). A little background music. *Principal, 71*(2), 41–44.

Gill, J. (1998). Jim Gill on music in the classroom. *Early Childhood Today, 12*(4), 36–39.

James, A. R. (2000). When I listen to the music. *Young Children, 55*(3), 36–37.

Snyder, S. (1997). Developing musical intelligence: Why and how. *Early Childhood Education Journal, 24*(3), 165–171.

Wilson, F. (1986). *Tone deaf & all thumbs? An introduction to music making.* New York: Random House.

Children's Books

Harper, B. M. (2002). *There was a bold lady who wanted a star.* Boston: Little, Brown.

Hoberman, M. A. (1998). *Miss Mary Mack.* Boston: Little, Brown.*

Hoberman, M. A. (2003). *Mary had a little lamb.* Boston: Little, Brown.

Hort, L. (2000). *The seals on the bus.* New York: Henry Holt.*

Kowalski, M. (1987). *The wheels on the bus.* Boston: Little, Brown.

Jackson, A. (1997). *I know an old lady who swallowed a pie.* New York: Puffin.

Sloat, T. (1998). *There was an old lady who swallowed a trout.* New York: Henry Holt.*

Trapani, I. (1993). *The itsy, bitsy spider.* Boston: Whispering Coyote Press.

Westcott, N. B. (1980). *I know an old lady who swallowed a fly.* Boston: Little, Brown.

Westcott, N. B. (1988). *The lady with the alligator purse.* Boston, Little, Brown.

Westcott, N. B. (1989). *Skip to my Lou.* Boston: Little, Brown.

*multicultural

TOURO COLLEGE LIBRARY

28 NAME-CALLING

CONCEPT

Why do some children call other children not-so-nice names? Where did they learn to do this? For many young children they first hear name-calling at home. Often older siblings love to tease their younger siblings by calling them names. Other children in the neighborhood or school may also be the culprits. Any time teasers find something that affects someone else they quickly put it to use. Essa (1990) notes:

> Children, like adults, want to feel good about themselves, so anything that does not reinforce a positive self-image is hurtful. The child who calls other children unpleasant names has found a way of hurting them. (p. 76)

The old saying that "sticks and stones may break my bones but names will never hurt me" is not true for most children. Names do hurt—but only when someone responds. If everyone ignores name-calling, it usually stops. If it does not, if this is a persistent problem among the children, you may want to learn more about the situation before it gets out of hand. Some questions you may want to consider include:

- How is the name-calling being done?
- Who calls and who is being called?
- What provokes the name-calling?
- When and where does it occur?
- How does the recipient respond?

Kindergarten and first grade children sometimes arrive at their own solutions to the name-calling problem at a class meeting. As Rightmyer (2003) tells us:

> Sometimes the class decided that the person called the name was empowered to take charge. "Just walk away" or "Make a joke of it." Other times, the name callers were reminded of their personal responsibility. (p. 42)

STEPS

1. **Ignore the name-calling and the caller yourself.**
2. **Help the recipient to ignore the name-calling.**
3. **Help the caller to understand how names hurt.**
4. **Read name-calling stories to both caller and recipient.**

ACTIVITIES

1. **Ignore the name-calling and the caller yourself.**

- You as a teacher can stop this inappropriate practice, first of all, by ignoring the name-caller yourself. He or she is asking for attention. Do not give it to him. Do not make eye contact

YOUNG COLLEGE LIBRARY

You should talk to the name-caller about the situation later after it is over.

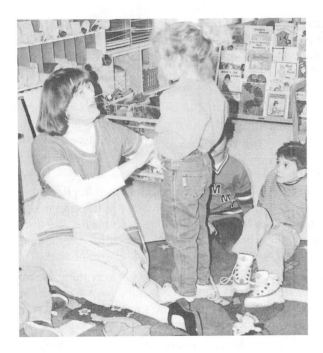

with the caller. Your own reaction as a teacher is just as important as the recipient's reaction. If you overreact and scold the caller or punish him, he only learns that such verbal aggression is a good way to get attention. As Hearron and Hildebrand (2005) note:

> Adult overreaction will only serve to teach children how powerful these words can be. Ignoring isolated occurrences will probably be much more effective than any long lecture about proper language. (p. 323)

- If the caller persists, you may have to lead him away and get him involved in some activity, still without making eye contact. You can talk to him about the situation later after it is over.

2. **Help the recipient to ignore the name-calling.**
   - Quietly tell the recipient of the name-calling not to look at or respond to the caller. Have the child turn her back and walk away. The caller and other children will see that you and the recipient are not bothered by the incident, and that you do not respond to the caller but only to the recipient. That sends a powerful message to someone who is calling for attention. The recipient will feel better because you came to her aid, while the caller and the others will see that he did not get your attention.

3. **Help the caller to understand how names hurt.**
   - Sometime later you can talk to the caller in a composed, not angry manner about name-calling, especially if this is something that has occurred before. Has this been done to him? How did he feel about it? How does he think the other child feels? Is there something he can say to make the other child feel better?

4. **Read name-calling stories to both caller and recipient.**
   - Sometimes name-calling is done for teasing, sometimes to get attention, and sometimes as aggression against another child. Can you tell what this case is about by looking at the caller's face or listening to the tone of his voice? If so, you may be able to decide which of the following books might help him best.

   Harry and Willy and Carrothead (Caseley, 1991)

   Emily Umily (Corrigan, 1991)

   Hurty Feelings (Lester, 2004)

   A Porcupine Named Fluffy (Lester, 1986)

   Eleanor, Ellatony, Ellencake, and Me (Rubin, 2003)

- *Harry and Willy and Carrothead* is a story about three friends at school: Harry, a boy who wears a prosthesis because he was born without a left hand; Willy, who likes to play baseball; and Oscar, whom Willy calls "carrothead" because of his orange hair. The name is not funny to Oscar but he doesn't say anything until Harry stands up for him and makes Willy stop. Talk to your listeners about nicknames, how they can be hurtful, and how they can be stopped.

- In *Emily Umily,* Emily is a little girl who dislikes kindergarten because the children make fun of her for saying "um" all the time. Finally they call her Umily. She finally overcomes her embarrassment by learning to chant "um" and teach the children to do it, too. Read this book to a recipient of name-calling who may be able to think of ways to help herself overcome her embarrassment.

- In *Hurty Feelings,* Fragility the Hippo has such fragile feelings that anything any of the other animals say to her, even nice things, make her flop to the ground and weep. But when Rudy a rude elephant tries to hurt her feelings on purpose, she holds her ground and makes him discover what it is like to have his feelings hurt. After reading this story, talk with the children about feelings: how they can be hurt—and also healed.

- Fluffy, in *A Porcupine Named Fluffy,* is not very fluffy, no matter how hard he tries to fluff himself up. Then one day he meets a rhinoceros who can't help laughing at Fluffy's name— that is until Fluffy finds out the rhino's name is Hippo! What a laugh for both of them. Can your children talk about why people should not laugh at other people's names?

- In *Eleanor, Ellatony, Ellencake, and Me*—these are all nicknames her family calls Ellen. She strongly objects to each of them and finally announces her own nickname: Ellie. What do your children think about nicknames?

REFERENCES AND SUGGESTED READINGS

Beaty, J. J. (1995). *Converting conflicts in preschool.* Clifton Park, NY: Thomson Delmar Learning.

Essa, E. L. (1990). *A practical guide to solving preschool behavior problems.* Clifton Park, NY: Thomson Delmar Learning.

Hearron, P., & Hildebrand, V. (2005). *Guiding young children.* Upper Saddle River, NJ: Merrill/Prentice Hall.

Rightmyer, E. C. (2003). Democratic discipline: Children creating solutions. *Young Children. 58*(4), 38–44.

Stone, J. (1993). Caregiver and teacher language—Responsive or restrictive? *Young Children. 48*(4), 12–18.

Children's Books

Caseley, J. (1991). *Harry and Willie and Carrothead.* New York: Greenwillow Books.

Corrigan, K. (1991). *Emily Umily.* Toronto: Annick Press.

Lester, H. (1986). *A porcupine named Fluffy.* Boston: Houghton Mifflin.

Lester, H. (2004). *Hurty feelings.* Boston: Houghton Mifflin.

Rubin, C. M. (2003). *Eleanor, Ellatony, Ellencake, and Me.* Columbus, OH: McGraw Hill.

29 NONVERBAL CUES

CONCEPT

Children look carefully at the adults around them to discover how the adults feel about them and what they are doing. You don't have to say a word. Your facial expressions including your eyes lighting up or darkening, your looks of delight or frowns, and your head positions of shaking or nodding say it all. These are called nonverbal cues, and are as important to young children as the words you say to them. They may not understand the words, but they understand your facial expressions and gestures. From birth on, young children have been observing the faces of their adult caregivers to interpret how their caregivers feel about them. As Greenspan (1999) notes:

> A child can sense, through facial expressions, vocal tones, and posture, how we feel about things. If we grit our teeth in exasperation but manage to say in a very controlled voice: "You're such a good child!" because we want to maintain a positive attitude, most children will sense the true emotions that underlie our words. (p. 366)

Body language is also a part of nonverbal communication. Coming close, bending over, squatting, touching, hugging, clapping hands, shaking hands, blowing kisses, and making victory signs with fingers are also common indications of people's feelings. Young children readily understand that a teacher is showing respect when he or she squats down to their eye level when talking to them instead of merely bending over.

This teacher shows respect for a child with the nonverbal cues of squatting down at the child's eye level and touching her arm.

It is no use for you to communicate to a child in an emotional situation with false words of praise when your nonverbal cues show the child just the opposite. As Greenspan (1999) continues: "When there's a conflict between the words a child hears and what he senses from our gestures, he will almost always believe the gestures" (p. 366).

When, then, should you use nonverbal cues with children? It is always important to show a smiling happy face when you first see individuals in the morning and when you say goodbye in the afternoon. There are several other times when nonverbal cues are especially meaningful to children:

- To help an attention-seeking child see that you are not angry at him but expect him to change his inappropriate behavior.
- During an emotional situation when you want to calm down a child but at the same time show her you are not angry with her.
- During an other-esteem conflict conversion situation between two children, when it is necessary for you to show your composure.
- To help improve a child's self-concept.

How can you learn to use nonverbal cues, and how do you know if you are really using them?

STEPS

1. **Have a "mirror day" in the classroom.**
2. **Have a "smile day" in the classroom.**
3. **Read books with faces that show emotions.**

ACTIVITIES

1. **Have a "mirror day" in the classroom.**
   - The idea behind having a "mirror day" in the classroom is to alert teachers and children to what they look like throughout the day. What are teachers' facial features showing when they must intervene in a conflict? When they speak to a child who is upsetting others? When they read a story? When they interact with individuals? What do children's features show, as well? Both teachers and children need to know what invisible (to them) information they are imparting to others.
   - Bring in many mirrors. You undoubtedly have a full-length mirror in the dramatic play center where children dress up and pretend. Place other mirrors here and there on the walls. Put several hand mirrors on top of dividers for teachers and children to pick up and look in from time to time.
   - Bring in several pocket mirrors for a small group activity at a table. Have each child look in the mirror and make a face. Have the others guess what kind of face each is making. You should participate, too.
   - When happy or not-so-happy incidents happen from time to time, ask children to look in one of the mirrors to see what feeling their face shows. Yours, too.

2. **Have a "smile day" in the classroom.**
   - You may tell the class that tomorrow will be a "smile day" and they should be prepared to put on a big smile when you give the signal. Or you may decide to hold an on-the-spot smile day when things are not going well or when everyone looks gloomy. A "smile day" can be anything you make it. Some teachers have a happy song they play now and then throughout the day as a signal for everyone to smile at everyone else. Or the signal for smiles can be jingle bells or playing on a triangle rhythm instrument or tap-tapping on a tambourine. When children hear it they need to stop doing what they are doing and turn and make a smile in the

Have a child look in a mirror to see what feeling his face is showing.

direction of someone. Stopping to smile usually ends up with everyone laughing or doing silly things.

- "Smile day" should also include some sort of surprise sometime during the day: perhaps a grab bag full of small toys for each child to reach in, or a paper party hat to wear, or funny stickers to put on faces, or making popcorn for a snack.
- Some teachers have their children draw a smiley picture of some kind to put up on their cubbies or take home. Have children think of something that makes them smile and draw it, like the picture in Figure 29–1.

3. Read books with faces that show emotions.

- *How Are You Peeling? Foods with Moods* (Freyman, 1999) is the perfect book to illustrate how faces show feelings. This is cleverly done with vegetables and fruits that pucker up or beam. An orange scowls, a pepper is sad, a tomato smiles. Can your children show any of these emotions?
- *Amazing Grace* (Hoffman, 1991) is a kindergarten girl who loves to pretend. The artist Caroline Binch draws her face showing excitement as Joan of Arc, wickedness as Anansi the

FIGURE 29–1 "I'm Smiling in My Garden and the Sun Is Smiling Too."

spider, sadness when she can't play Peter Pan and smiling wonder when she does. What can your children pretend to be with their faces?

- *Please, Baby, Please* (Lee & Lee, 2002) shows an African American baby getting into all kinds of mischief with smiling, smirking faces to go along. How would your children show it if they poured their cereal on their heads?
- In *Alligator Baby* (Munsch, 1997) Kristen's cartoon-character mother and father get mixed up and go to the zoo instead of the hospital when her mother has her baby, and end up bringing home a series of animal babies. Finally Kristen goes and finds her real human brother in with a gorilla. Cartoon faces show exaggerated features on all of the characters, including the animals. Have your children try making them, too.

REFERENCES AND SUGGESTED READINGS

Beaty, J. J. (2004). *Skills for preschool teahcers* (7th ed.). Upper Saddle River, NJ: Merill/Prentice Hall.

Ferber, J. (1996). A look in the mirror: Self-concept in preschool children. In L. Koplow (Ed.), *Unsmiling faces: How preschools can heal.* New York: Teachers College Press.

Greenspan, S. (1999). *Building Healthy Minds.* New York: Da Capo Press.

Hearron, P. F., & Hildebrand, V. (2005). *Guiding young children* (7th ed.). Upper Saddle River, NJ: Merrill/Prentice Hall.

Hyson, M. (2004). *The emotional development of young children: Building an emotion-centered curriculum* (2nd ed.). New York: Teachers College Press.

Kontos, S., & Wilcox-Herzog, A. (1997). Teachers' interactions with children: Why are they so important? *Young Children, 52*(2), 4–12.

Children's Books

Freyman, S. (1999). *How are you peeling? Foods with moods.* New York: Alfred A. Levine Books.

Hoffman, M. (1991). *Amazing Grace.* New York: Dial Books.*

Lee, S., & Lee T. L. (2002). *Please, baby, please.* New York: Simon & Schuster.*

Munsch, D. (1997). *Alligator baby.* New York: Scholastic, Inc.

───────

*multicultural

30 OTHER-ESTEEM

CONCEPT

Young children are born to be egocentric, that is, self-centered. This is part of the survival mechanism of all human beings. From infancy on, children tend to be concerned with themselves alone until a new sibling comes into the family or until they enter a child care program or preschool. At this point they are faced with the fact that they are not the center of attention any more. Many children have trouble accepting this fact and may struggle to try to gain their former position.

Many families try to help their young children understand that there are others like themselves who also need attention. Families who succeed in opening the minds of their young children to the needs of others still younger are generally those who secure the youngsters' help in caring for their littler siblings. This tends to happen more often in large families where the next older sibling is expected to help care for the younger one. If they do not understand this new role, their older siblings soon impress it on them.

But many children entering preschool are still very self-centered, expecting everything to revolve around them as it did at home. The wonderland of toys they see in the classroom is surely for them alone. The idea of sharing and taking turns is not a part of their awareness at first. They are not attuned to "other-esteem."

Other-esteem is a feeling of empathy for another person. It is an awareness that another child may feel the same as she does. She may be angry if someone takes her toy. He may be upset if another child intrudes in his space. If a child can recognize that the other child has feelings, too, we say he is developing "other-esteem."

The conflict conversion strategy discussed in chapter 6: Conflict Conversion asks each child involved in a two-party conflict to tell how the other child feels. This is something new for most children. They know how *they* feel. Why should they be concerned about the other child? But when the teacher asks them to look at the other child's face and tell how they think the other child feels, they may see tears or anger that means the other child feels as bad as they do. This is other-esteem. Ramsey (1991) believes that young children can really feel this about others:

> Because even very young children resonate to others' emotions, children can empathize and communicate on an emotional plane before they are consciously aware of others' perspectives. (p. 18)

For children to become truly "socialized" in our society they need to be able to empathize with others. They need to be able to see beyond their own self-interests and recognize that others also have interests that need to be respected. As teachers we are too often concerned with children's self-esteem: that they feel good about themselves. Just as important is children's other-esteem: that they feel good about others. How many children in your class have any kind of feeling at all about the child next to her?

Developing other-esteem can truly make a difference in children and their behavior in the classroom. They may begin to understand *why* they should share toys and take turns with equipment, and *why* they should not hit someone or knock down someone's block building. This is not something you teach a child directly. It is something they learn through their interactions with others and your facilitation of it.

"How do you think Rachel feels, Haley, when you take her doll? What does her face tell you?" And to Rachel you might say: "How do you think Haley feels, Rachel, when you hit her? What does her face tell you?" As children experience other-esteem conflict conversion questions like this, they begin to see things from another child's perspective. They may eventually begin to take this into account before acting as they did in the past. You will need to talk with them about other-esteem—that it means showing concern for another person, not just for yourself. Other-esteem is the opposite of being selfish.

Here are some other means you can use to help children develop other-esteem as a strategy for promoting positive guidance.

STEPS

1. **Have two puppets enact an other-esteem scenario.**
2. **Have other-esteem stickers.**
3. **Read stories with other-esteem themes.**

ACTIVITIES

1. **Have two puppets enact an other-esteem scenario.**
   - Put two puppets on your hands (Dominick and Justin) and role-play a brief scenario with both of them for a small group of children who have had trouble recognizing the rights of others. Pretend Dominick is sitting at the computer and Justin is waiting impatiently for a turn. Justin keeps after him to finish but Dominick ignores him. Finally the Justin puppet pulls Dominick away and they both struggle.
   - Have children talk about what happened and whether either of the puppets showed other-esteem. How should they each have acted if they wanted to show other-esteem? Replay the scene with the puppets acting as the children have decided they should act. Then give the puppets to two children and help them enact a similar scene. Did either puppet show other-esteem?

2. **Have other-esteem stickers.**
   - In order to bring the idea of other-esteem to the children's attention, you need to point out children who perform unselfish acts as well as those who show concern for another person. Some teachers like to use "other-esteem stickers." You can ask a child to put a sticker on another child who is performing an unselfish act. No fair letting children put a sticker on themselves when they do something unselfish—that in itself is being selfish. Someone else must see the act and place the sticker. Children can even put a sticker on a puppet who shows other-esteem!
   - If we want children to show concern for other children, it is important to talk about other-esteem, to point it out when we see it happening, and to thank the children who perform the other-esteem acts by acknowledging them with something like a sticker.

Zachary gives Albert the truck he wanted without being asked—an other-esteem act.

3. **Read stories with other-esteem themes.**

- Children will learn to show concern for others and their feelings only if this theme is integrated into the classroom in many ways. Reading books with other-esteem themes and talking about them afterward is an important way to keep this topic in the forefront of children's thinking. Many children's picture books feature other-esteem themes of one character helping another—or not helping another, but you must look for them. The idea of other-esteem is not at the forefront of most people's thinking. You and your children can help change things. Have them find the other-esteem acts in these books.

- *I Am Too Absolutely Small for School* (Child, 2004) and *I Will Never Not Ever Eat a Tomato* (Child, 2000) are two outstanding books about inventive big brother Charlie and his concerns for his obstinate little sister Lola, written in the off-beat ideas and language of childhood. When Lola objects to going to school because she already can count to 10, Charlie asks her (with marvelous illustrations) what she would do if eleven eager elephants all wanted a treat? In the *Tomato* book Lola continues her objections about eating anything, even her mashed potatoes, until Charlie points out that they are cloud fluff from the pointiest peak of Mt. Fuji! Both of these books make excellent sources for children's reenactments and discussion of other-esteem.

- In *Hide and Seek Turkeys* (Enderle & Gordon, 2004) costumed children put on a play in rhyme about ten turkeys that hide from a fox one-by-one in old-fashioned clothing found in a farmhouse. But there is never enough room and one is always left out. Can your children decide how other-esteem enters this picture?

- In *Jamaica's Find* (Havill, 1986) the little African American girl Jamaica finds a stuffed dog toy on the playground and takes it home instead of turning it in to Lost and Found. She wants to keep it but finally, with mother's help, decides to turn it in just as another little girl turns up who lost the dog. Can Jamaica's act count as other-esteem?

- *Clarabella's Teeth* (Vrombaut, 2003) shows the cartoon animals Ruby the rabbit, Liam the leopard, Max the monkey, and Zoe the zebra all brushing their teeth and running out to play. But poor Clarabella crocodile is still brushing, brushing, brushing her enormous mouthful of crocodile teeth until playtime is over. Finally Ruby solves the problem with a huge surprise from her friends: a crocodile toothbrush! Was this other-esteem? Gilchrist (1994), who originated the term *other-esteem,* has this question to ask us:

  If one has been continually self-absorbed, self-focused, and self-contained, can he or she develop a working concept of 'other'? Perhaps, as we are developing esteem for ourselves or teaching it to others, we can balance these ideas and concepts with considering the esteem for others. (p. 2)

REFERENCES AND SUGGESTED READINGS

Beaty, J. J. (1999). *Prosocial guidance for the preschool child.* Upper Saddle River, NJ: Merrill/Prentice Hall.

Camras, L. A. (1980). Children's understanding of facial expressions during conflict encounters. *Child Development, 51,* 879–885.

Gilchrist, M. A. (1994). Other-esteem: Society's missing link? (unpublished manuscript). Columbia, MO: Central Missouri Foster Grandparent Program.

Greenspan, S. (2000). *Building healthy minds.* New York: Da Capo Press.

Hoffman, M. L. (1982). Development of prosocial motivation: Empathy and guilt. In N. Eisenberg (Ed.), *The development of prosocial behavior.* New York: Teachers College Press.

Ramsey, P. G. (1991). *Making friends in school: Promoting peer relationships in early childhood.* New York: Teachers College Press.

Children's Books

Child, L. (2000). *I will never not ever eat a tomato.* Cambridge, MA: Candlewick Press.

Child, L. (2004). *I am too absolutely small for school.* Cambridge, MA: Candlewick Press.

Enderle, J. R., & Gordon, S. J. (2004). *Hide and seek turkeys.* New York: Margaret K. McElderry Books.

Havill, J. (1986). *Jamaica's find.* Boston: Houghton Mifflin.*

Vrombaut, A. (2003). *Clarabella's teeth.* New York: Clarion Books.

———
*multicultural

31

PLAY, DRAMATIC

CONCEPT

All young children learn through play. Play, in fact, is their primary vehicle for learning how people, things, and the world around them work. Pioneer child development theorist Vygotsky believed that play was extremely important in child development in ways that are not always obvious. Bodrova and Leong (1996) tell us:

> For Vygotsky, play serves as a tool of the mind enabling children to master their own behavior. The imaginary situations created in play are the first constraints that channel and direct behavior in a specific way. Play organizes behavior. Instead of producing totally spontaneous behavior, in play the child acts like a mommy or like a truck driver, for example. (p. 125)

The type of play referred to is pretend play, carried on in early childhood classrooms as "dramatic play" or "sociodramatic play." One of the most important learning centers in such early childhood classrooms is the dramatic play center where child-size furniture, adult dress-up clothes, and props promote children's acting out of roles and scenarios of their own choosing. They may pretend to be mommy, daddy, baby, or brother during an early morning episode of their own invention. Police officers, firefighters, and doctors often make an appearance when children have concerns about unsettling situations in the world around them. Teachers often furnish particular props to help children integrate their impressions of field trips taken to a doctor's office, fire station, supermarket, construction site, or zoo.

Dramatic play can also serve as an excellent guidance strategy to help children work through the fears they may have such as visiting the doctor or moving to a new community. When disturbing events touch the children's world, dramatic play can be used as a therapeutic release of emotions. How does it work?

Small groups of children may choose to play in the dramatic play center whenever the daily schedule allows it. They make up their own scenarios about things that interest or concern them. One or more children may be directors who determine the theme or assign roles. Or children may automatically take on their own roles. If teachers have furnished particular props, suggested certain themes, or read books to motivate them, children may follow these ideas in their pretend play.

Favorite themes are often played out over and over on different days with children trying out various roles. Children may be directors or role-players as the episodes evolve, or both at the same time, giving directions while following directions given to them. All of this seems to happen spontaneously as children switch roles, negotiate for new roles, or go off on their own.

For you as a teacher hoping to use dramatic play as a vehicle for guiding children in emotional situations, you should first observe children during their normal dramatic play episodes to see how they handle this pretending. Remember that this type of play is the children's own, and as a teacher you should rarely become involved as a player. You can help them get started with their play if necessary. But then you need to withdraw and let them continue on their own. If they are working through emotional scenarios, you may want to talk with them afterward, or if the play stalls, you may want to suggest new directions for it. But your best role is to observe and record what is happening and what children seem to be learning from the play. (See Figure 31–1.)

FIGURE 31–1
Observation Form for
"Going to the Doctor's."

1. What do child patients think will happen?
2. How do they express what they think (actions, words, nonverbal cues)?
3. How do they express fear (or other emotions)?
4. What do they think about the nurse?
5. How does the nurse treat the patients?
6. What do they think about the doctor?
7. How does the doctor treat the patients?
8. How does the episode end?

A most important finding that teacher-observers have discovered is that "play makes visible children's thinking" (Roskos & Christie, 2001, p. 66). As Hatcher and Petty (2004) discuss in their article *Seeing Is Believing: Visible Thought in Dramatic Play,*

> *Viewing play not just as an activity, but as an expression of thinking, lets adults begin to appreciate how children understand their world. As children play they establish important links between action and thought, connections that are the basis of mental processes.* (p. 79)

If you as a teacher can discover through observing children in dramatic play what they are thinking and learning about themselves and their world, you can make your guidance strategies more meaningful. Here are steps that may help.

STEPS

1. Observe children during dramatic play to learn what they understand about the theme.
2. Talk with the children about their feelings, or have them express their feelings through art.
3. Read children's books about the theme they are playing and discuss what they think the book characters learned.

ACTIVITIES

1. Observe children during dramatic play to learn what they understand about the theme.

- Figure 31–1 asks you to answer several questions about what you see happening during a pretend episode of "going to the doctor's." Look for actions, dialog, and nonverbal communication.

- One teacher observed a brief, spontaneous dramatic play episode of "going to the doctor's" in which three children were involved: Adalina, the mother; Cecily, the nurse; and Andrew, the doctor. The dramatic play center was arranged with an "examining" table and three chairs to one side. Adalina sat on a chair holding a baby doll. Cecily came, took the baby doll, and put it on the examining table. Adalina got up quickly and took back the doll. Cecily took the doll again and put it on the table, saying: "The doctor needs to examine your baby." Adalina, becoming anxious, said: "Will it hurt?" Noticing the baby was lying unclothed on the table, she rushed over to a crib nearby, got a blanket, and covered the doll. Andrew came in with a "ballpoint-pen-hypodermic-needle" to give the baby a shot. Adalina grabbed up the doll again saying, "Don't hurt my baby!" and left the area with the doll.

- This typical episode had often been enacted in this classroom, sometimes with more "mothers" with dolls waiting to be examined, sometimes with a "mother" taking a real child by the hand to be examined. Sometimes the mothers allowed their babies to get a shot, sometimes not. The class had visited a well-baby clinic and was impressed with the order of events that had taken place:

  1. Mothers signing in at a reception desk.
  2. Mothers (and one father) sitting in the waiting room with their babies waiting for their name to be called.
  3. Mothers going into an examining room.
  4. Nurses weighing, taking temperatures, asking questions, talking to the baby, and helping prepare the baby for the exam.
  5. Doctors coming in quickly, talking to the mother and baby briefly, examining the baby and writing notes, then leaving. (No shots were given.)

- Most interesting was the fact that the children seemed to think that the nurse, not the doctor, was in charge. In their play, the director of the scenario was always the nurse. Also although no shots were given, almost all the children's scenarios included a "shot scene," sometimes with pretend crying. These children were reenacting their own experiences of getting shots. They always showed nervousness about it, even in pretend.

2. **Talk with the children about their feelings, or have them express their feelings through art.**

- It was obvious to the teachers that going to the doctor's was a traumatic event for the children, whether or not shots were given. The children really did not want to talk about it, but they would paint pictures about it and reenact the scene many times in pretend play. Dramatic play was definitely a catharsis. Eventually the play theme petered out, but every now and then a few children would dramatize it again. It never really lost its popularity in the doll corner when children discovered a toy thermometer they could use for giving baby dolls a "shot."

This "mother" is thinking about giving her "baby" a shot.

3. **Read children's books about the theme they are playing and discuss what they think the book characters learned.**

   - Teachers found that reading books *after* the field trip and the dramatic play episodes produced the best results. It was then that the children would talk about the trauma of getting shots or being examined. When children compared these stories with the real thing, teachers then learned what the children actually understood about the concept of going to the doctor's. The three most popular books on the subject turned out to be:

   This Is a Hospital, Not a Zoo! (Karim, 1998)

   Froggy Goes to the Doctor (London, 2002)

   How Do Dinosaurs Get Well Soon? (Yolen, 2003)

   All three are hilarious take-offs on the real thing, and the children by then knew what the real thing entailed, which makes them all the funnier.

   - *This Is a Hospital, Not a Zoo!* is the riotous adventure of Filbert McFee, a boy who finds himself in a hospital under the strict control of Head Nurse Beluga, but who longs desperately to go home. A package of animal crackers arrives just as he is about to get a shot, and he pops one into his mouth, turning him into a rhino with thick skin! At the cold X-ray station he pops in another cracker and turns into a penguin. When it's time for his medicine he turns into a giraffe with his mouth out of reach, and then an orangutan. The only solution? Send Filbert McFee home! The story will send your listeners into spasms of laughter. Bring in the animal crackers and have each child recipient tell how he felt when he got a shot, had an X-ray, or had to take medicine. After hearing this story your dramatic doctor play should turn into something different, too!

   - In *Froggy Goes to the Doctor* little boy Froggy is so nervous in the waiting room he falls off a bench, makes a paper airplane that hits Dr. Mugwort in the eye, forgets to brush his teeth, forgets to put on underwear, and kicks the poor doctor on the floor when she tests his reflexes. She pulls out her gigantic needle for his shot, but she is only teasing. He is fine and very healthy. Have your listeners relate their experiences at the doctor's after they finish laughing.

   - In *How Do Dinosaurs Get Well Soon?* giant pictures of cantankerous dinosaurs show how they might resist everything a doctor or nurse tries to get them to do. But that isn't how they really act, and they demonstrate in rhyme how they actually behave. How would your children behave in each of these situations? Read the book to a small group and have the children pantomime the dinosaurs' actions. Can they do it without laughing?

REFERENCES AND SUGGESTED READINGS

Bodrova, E., & Leong, D. J. (1996). *Tools of the mind: The Vygotskian approach to early childhood education.* Upper Saddle River, NJ: Merrill/Prentice Hall.

Cooper, J. L., & Dever, M. T. (2001). Sociodramatic play as a vehicle for curriculum intergration in first grade. *Young Children, 56*(3), 58–63.

Cummins, L. (2004). The funeral of Froggy the Frog: The child as dramatist, designer, and realist. *Young Children, 59*(4), 87–91.

Hatcher, B., & Petty, K. (2004). Seeing is believing: Visible thought in dramatic play. *Young Children, 59*(6), 79–82.

Roskos, K., & Christie, J. (2001). Not pushing too hard: A few cautionary remarks about linking literacy and play. *Young Children, 56*(3), 64–66.

Children's Books

Karim, R. (1998). *This is a hospital, not a zoo!* New York: Clarion Books.

London, J. (2002). *Froggy goes to the doctor.* New York: Viking.

Yolen, J. (2003). *How do dinosaurs get well soon?* New York: Blue Sky Press.

32

PLAY, SUPERHERO

CONCEPT

Young children are being bombarded with scenes of violence, war, and combat everywhere you turn these days. Action toys, video games, movies, cartoons, news programs, and sporting events all show people fighting. Toy departments are full of realistic stun guns, lasers, rifles, water pistols, swords, shields, military tanks, planes, and rockets—along with the warriors and action figures to use this equipment. Why shouldn't young children, especially boys, bring some of these ideas and material into the classroom? Why shouldn't their pretend play include aggressive acts toward one another with superheroes out to save the world from the bad guys?

Teachers can try to ban guns, war play, and superheroes from the classroom, but children who are determined to play out scenes from the violent television they watch will find ways to circumvent the ban. No guns in the classroom? Then children will use unit blocks as guns, build their own from Legos, or simply use their fingers. As Levin (2003a) notes:

> Children find ways to circumvent the ban—they deny that play is really war play (that is, they learn to lie) or sneak around conducting guerilla wars the teacher does not detect (they learn to deceive). (p. 61)

We understand that young children have a great need to work through strong emotions, in this instance, fear: fear of what the bad guys might do to them; fear of people with guns shooting them or blowing them up. Superheroes, on the other hand, seem to offer them a means for overcoming this violence and its perpetrators, since nothing can hurt a superhero.

Yet in the classroom, superhero play generally includes aggressiveness and violence itself as the superheroes crush the bad guys. Even though children are only pretending, pretending to hurt others is not what teachers have in mind. Using aggressiveness to stop violence is not what children should be learning about solving problems. Teachers who allow a limited form of superhero play seem to spend much of their time trying to the control it and keep the play within established limits. In fact, most war and superhero play usually ends in crying and someone getting hurt. What, then, should teachers do when they believe that children should be allowed to pretend on their own and work through emotional situations? As Levin (2003b) tells us:

> Children need help from adults in working through the issues raised by violent and disturbing content in the media. Merely banning the play does not give children the help they need and can even increase the harmful impact of the violence. (p. 83)

When violent superhero play occurs and someone gets hurt, teachers need to take the players aside and talk to them about the roles they are acting out. What caused the bad guys to be bad? What powers does the superhero have that can be used to stop the bad guys nonviolently? What else can the superheroes do with their powers to help others?

For pretend play to be meaningful, it needs to be controlled by the players, not the teacher, as discussed in chapter 31: Dramatic Play. But it also needs to be creative and not imitative: something the children invent themselves and not just copy from a television program. Instead of banning superhero play you can help your children create a substitute for it that is just as powerful and satisfying. You can motivate them to design a new kind of superhero play based on using the superhero's powers in a positive way. You can also scale down the play using miniature superhero figures in the block center or sand table. In addition, you can set up art projects for them to paint a superhero picture and dictate a story about it, or model in clay or play dough superhero weapons that don't hurt people.

Think of other ways you can engage children's creativity in inventing their own superheroes with positive powers. Does anyone suggest having a Music Man whose power is in the magic verse he sings or flute he plays to disarm robbers or stop bad guys? Children can dictate stories about the superheroes that they can later reenact. Use your own creativity to help the children use theirs.

STEPS

1. **Use a miniature version of some of the children's superheroes and make up new scenarios.**
2. **Convert some of the children's book characters to superheroes and act out new scenarios.**
3. **Paint pictures of superheroes and make up new stories about them.**
4. **Create animal superheroes and make up scenarios for them to help save the world.**

ACTIVITIES

1. **Use a miniature version of some of the children's superheroes and make up new scenarios.**
   - For example, obtain a small figure of Spiderman (or a laminated cutout), string, tacks, and a large piece of cardboard, corkboard, or a bulletin board. Put pictures of buildings on the board. Place tacks on the pictures and around the board and string the string from one tack to another creating a "spider web" for Spiderman to cling to. Use several small figures or cutouts of people along with Spiderman to play on this board. Have children invent their own scenarios or use some like: "How Spiderman Helps Banks to Keep Robbers from Stealing Money," or "How Spiderman Helps the Police to Prevent Crimes."
   - Convert miniature block people figures to superheroes by fastening a little cape to their backs so they can "fly." Each child can make his own. Name the new superheroes and decide on what positive powers they have. Children can play with them in elaborate scenarios in the block center or at the sand table.

2. **Convert some of the children's book characters to superheroes and act out new scenarios.**
   - The African folktale *Abiyoyo* (Seeger, 1994) introduces listeners to two wonderful superheroes: a boy and his father. Although they look like ordinary people, they possess two superpowers. The father has a magic wand that can make people disappear, but they have to be lying down. The boy has a magic ukulele that can make people dance. A giant named Abiyoyo is terrorizing their village and eating people. Together the boy and his father approach the giant monster, and the boy starts playing. The giant dances until he falls down exhausted. The father quickly goes zoop! with his wand and the giant disappears forever. Your children can become these two super characters in their dramatic play with a stick wand and a shoe box banjo. The rest of the class can sing the song "Abiyoyo."
   - Grace from the book *Amazing Grace* (Hoffman, 1991) can make an amazing superhero by turning herself into one of the characters from the story (Joan of Arc, Anansi the Spider, Peg Leg the pirate, Hiawatha, Mowgli the jungle boy, or Aladdin with his magic lamp). Your listeners can decide what superpowers these characters should possess, then dress up like Grace did and act out wonderful scenarios about them.
   - *Kapow!* (O'Connor, 2004) is a new book about two children pretending to be superheroes: American Eagle and Bug Lady. They say the words "fwoosh" and "zoom" as they go about saving the world in their own house. But they get a bit carried away trying to capture Rubber Bandit (little brother), and knock down a bookcase. After reading this book, be sure to talk about how superheroes can sometimes get carried away with their powers, and then what happens.

This boy is deciding which block figure he will convert to a superhero of his own by fastening a cape to its back.

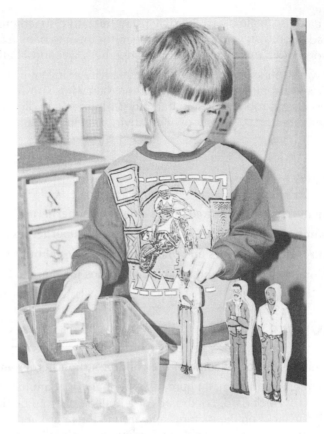

3. **Paint pictures of superheroes and make up new stories about them.**
   - Once children have agreed to make their superheroes more positive and less destructive, they can appear in any center of the classroom including art. After a healthy food discussion one boy painted the "before" and "after" picture in Figure 32–1.

4. **Create animal superheroes and make up scenarios for them to help save the world.**
   - Any of the stuffed animals in your program can be converted to superheroes. By now the children will have the idea of putting a cape on them so they can fly. Even though children

FIGURE 32–1 "If I Eat Apples, Oranges, Grapes, and Bananas, It Makes Me Big Like the Hulk."

seem more interested in human superheroes, the children may be attracted to a book animal character with extraordinary powers. *Zomo the Rabbit* (McDermott, 1992) is another African folktale about a rabbit who is not big, not strong, but he is very clever.

REFERENCES AND SUGGESTED READINGS

Boyatzis, C. J. (1997). Of Power Rangers and V-chips. *Young Children, 52*(7), 74–79.

Carlsson-Paige, N., & Levin, D. E. (1987). *The war play dilemma: Balancing needs and values in the early childhood classroom.* New York: Teachers College Press.

Johnston, J. M. (1987). Harnessing the power of superheroes: An alternative view. *Day Care and Early Education. 15*(1), 15–17.

Levin, D. E. (2003a). Beyond banning war and superhero play: Meeting children's needs in violent times. *Young Children, 58*(3), 60–63.

Levin, D. E. (2003b). *Teaching young children in violent times.* Washington, DC: National Association for the Education of Young Children.

Pena, S., French, J., & Holmes, R. (1987). A look at superheroes: Some issues and guidelines. *Day Care and Early Education, 15*(1), 10–14.

Children's Books

Hoffman, M. (1991). *Amazing Grace.* New York: Dial Books.*

McDermott, G. (1992). *Zomo the Rabbit: A Trickster Tale from West Africa.* San Diego: Harcourt.*

O'Connor, G. (2004). *Kapow!* New York: Simon & Schuster.

Seeger, P. (1994). *Abiyoyo.* New York: Aladdin Paperbacks.*

_____

*multicultural

33 POWER STRUGGLES

CONCEPT

Although most children ages 3, 4, 5, and 6 are still dependent upon adults for nearly everything in their lives, some are struggling fiercely for autonomy—for independence and control of what goes on around them. They may be the ones who want to take charge of the dramatic play scenarios, the block building structures, the computer programs, and the favorite toys. They may even challenge you on the limits you set and the way you want them to behave. Much of their lives, in fact, may revolve around such power struggles.

While their first struggles in your program may have been over the possession of toys, as they grow older, they shift to issues of control. They want the first turn, the biggest piece, and the best toy. But especially, they want to be in control of others. Other children should play the way they demand, take the pretend roles they assign, or build the block buildings their way. When their peers object, a struggle ensues. Shantz (1987) found that the largest percentage of preschoolers' conflicts involve object possession, but as they grow older the second largest category of conflicts involves control of another child's actions or lack of actions.

> As children get older, an increasingly smaller proportion of the conflicts are about the physical environment (e.g. objects and space), and an increasingly larger proportion concern control of the "social environment." (p. 287)

Step back and observe what is happening in your classroom. What kinds of conflicts do you see? If the conflicts seem to be about control of another child's actions, you may be witnessing a power struggle. Unless the conflict results in crying or physically hurting someone, the usual role of the teacher is to let the children work out their own resolutions rather than intervening. However, in the case of power struggles, if you note that one child always wins control over others by threatening or bullying, you need to step in. Some children have unfortunately learned that the way to get what they want is by using bully tactics and making others afraid of them. You can change this by helping power-seekers find more peaceful means to gain power, by helping other children to resist power seekers, and still others to overcome their fear of bullies.

First of all, do not let yourself be drawn into a struggle with the power-seeking child. As Marion (2003) tells us: "Engaging in a power struggle with a child makes a child's power-seeking behavior even stronger" (p. 346). When you feel that this is happening, simply decline to engage with him or her. Tell the child you do not want to argue or fight with him and then leave. You may then want to try these steps:

STEPS

1. **Help power-seekers overcome their need to control by putting them in charge of something special.**
2. **Help other children to resist the actions of power-seekers, and power-seekers to change.**
3. **Help certain children to overcome the fear of bullies.**

ACTIVITIES

1. **Help power-seekers overcome their need to control by putting them in charge of something special.**

   - First you need to talk with the child involved in a power-struggle about what he or she is doing. The other-esteem conflict conversion method has a place here. (See chapter 6: Conflict Conversion.) You should definitely ask this child first how the other child feels about what has happened, and then ask the other child how the power-seeker feels. This is such a surprising approach, the power-seeker may comply when he sees he is not being blamed. It may be the first time he has been asked to consider another child's feelings or have another child consider his. After the two children decide on how to make one another feel better, you can decide whether this may be the time to read a book about a power-seeker.

   - Before putting a power-seeker in charge of something special, he should hear at least one story about another power-seeker: in this case Pinkerton, the pig. Pinkerton in *Me First* (Lester, 1992) would do anything to be first (and most powerful), even if it meant stepping on snouts or tying tails. When his scout troop goes to the beach for a picnic he hears someone call: "Who would care for a sandwich?" He rushes forward first, only to find to his chagrin that the caller is a "sand witch" who makes Pinkerton care for her—until he learns his lesson. Talk with your own power-seeker about this lesson.

   - The "something special" one teacher designed for her power-seekers was to be in charge of special collections in their science area. They had visited a museum and learned the names of scientists in charge of different displays of insects, dinosaur bones, fishes, and butterflies. The names intrigued the children and they wanted to use them in their own science displays:

     Entomologist: bug collector

     Paleontologist: dinosaur displayer

     Ichthyologist: fish feeder

     Lepidopterist: butterfly hatcher

     Geologist: rock collector

     Could 4-year-olds pronounce such words? Yes, and they gloried in it. Each child who was appointed to be in charge of a display wore the name on a yarn necklace and had a daily chore to perform. They were powerful positions and children who were appointed knew they could not seek power elsewhere.

2. **Help other children to resist the actions of power-seekers, and power-seekers to change.**

   - Teachers can sometimes help submissive children to resist the demands of a power-seeker by teaching them to use some of these strategies:

     1. Tell him "no."
     2. Give a reason for not complying.
     3. Make a counterproposal.
     4. Walk away to another activity.

   - It is not always easy to change this sort of behavior because some children are more or less submissive by nature, and some power-seekers do not know how else to act. Other strategies that sometimes work include: a) putting the power-seeker in a small group of assertive children where she must let others have their way or else negotiate, or b) putting the power-seeker and submissive child in a small group where everyone has a turn to be "boss."

3. **Help certain children to overcome the fear of bullies.**

   - Some children allow others to dominate them because they are afraid to resist. You may never know who they are because the fearful child gives in to the bully immediately. Timid children need your help in learning to stand up to a bully. If you have timid or shy children in your class, watch to see whether they are being bothered by an aggressive child. If so, you can help them by working with them one-on-one.

This boy, the "entomologist," is in charge of the class's plastic insect collection, as well as collecting live insects.

- Read the timid child a book like *Bootsie Barker Bites* (Bottner, 1992) about the poor little girl narrator who is scared to death when Bootsie comes to her house to play. Bootsie man-handles the girl while pretending to be a dinosaur who will bite her. Next time the girl tells her mother, who advises her to play a different game. She turns off the lights in her room with only a flash lantern to throw dark shadows on the wall, and declares to Bootsie with a flourish that she is a paleontologist who hunts for dinosaur bones. Bootsie screams and runs for the door. What can your child say to turn the tables on her tormentor? Can you help her?

- Sometimes a bully's ways can be overcome if those he is trying to control simply walk away and won't play with him. In the book *This Is Our House* (Rosen, 1996), George takes over the cardboard carton house on the playground and won't let the other children in no matter what they try. They wait for their chance and eventually George has to go to the bathroom, at which point all the children crowd into the house. When George returns he shouts and kicks and stamps his feet to no avail. But finally he decides this is a house for everyone, and they let him in. Do reading books like this really help? Ramsey (1991) along with this author believes:

    Children's books are a primary vehicle for this kind of teaching. By engaging children in stories, we enable our young readers and listeners to empathize with different experiences and points of view and experience a wide range of social dilemmas. (p. 168)

REFERENCES AND SUGGESTED READINGS

Beaty, J. J. (1995). *Converting conflicts in preschool.* Clifton Park, NY: Thomson Delmar Learning.
Marion, M. (2003). *Guidance of young children* (6th ed.). Upper Saddle River, NJ: Merrill/Prentice Hall.
Ramsey, P. G. (1991). *Making friends in school: Promoting peer relationships in early childhood.* New York: Teachers College Press.
Shantz, C. U. (1987). Conflicts between children. *Child Development, 58,* 283–305.

Children's Books
Bottner, B. (1992). *Bootsie Barker bites.* New York: Putnam's.
Lester, H. (1992). *Me first.* Boston: Houghton Mifflin.
Rosen, M. (1996). *This is our house.* Cambridge, MA: Candlewick Press.*

*multicultural

34   PRAISE

CONCEPT

Teachers who are familiar with research in early childhood guidance know there is a serious concern about teachers using praise as a strategy. Automatic praise such as "good job" or "I like it" or "What a beautiful picture" may not convey to young children what teachers think it does. As Wolfgang (2004) notes:

> Praise such as "good job" is widely used by adults who believe that they are being positive and supportive. In reality, based on knowledge about children's moral development (Piaget, 1965), adults who praise may be teaching children to be dependent and thus stifling children's abilities to be self-motivated and make their own judgments. (p. 7)

Children, on the other hand, need to connect with teachers and have them respond to what they are doing and creating. What does "good job" or "what a beautiful painting" really tell children? If you use it automatically for every child every day, it probably says little more than "I see what you have done." That may satisfy children if they are looking for your attention, but most youngsters want something more. They want a statement that helps them evaluate their behavior or work. They are looking for *encouragement*.

With art work we understand it is the process that is most important to young children, not the product. Thus a painting that looks like a giant brown smudge may not be really "beautiful" either to you or to the child, but may represent long minutes of difficult work using every color available. What should your response be when a child shows you this painting? The sensitive teacher does not say, "It's beautiful" or "I like it," if this is not how she feels. Instead, she uses a statement of encouragement such as, "Oh, Melanie, you really worked hard with your painting this morning. What do you think?" Or she might be even more specific, saying: "I see red and blue and green in your painting. What other colors did you use?" While praise is an external value, encouragement helps a child recognize her own efforts as she sees it.

But what about motivating behavior, you may wonder? Doesn't praise motivate children to act in a positive manner? When you are trying to help children learn to share toys or take turns without a fuss, shouldn't you praise them when they do these things? Doesn't praise motivate them? Kohn (2001) says: "Sure. It motivates them to get praise . . . often at the expense of commitment to whatever they were doing that prompted the praise" (p. 26).

How then are teachers to act if they can no longer say "good job" or "good trying" or "good helping"? For some teachers these words are just as automatic as saying, "Have a good day." What can teachers do to break this automatic praise habit?

STEPS

1. **Have a praise-conversion session.**
2. **Look at children's art with new eyes.**
3. **Use "specific praise" privately to encourage children's positive behavior.**

ACTIVITIES

1. **Have a praise-conversion session.**

   - Breaking a habit is not all that easy—especially a "saying" habit. But if you are serious in cutting down on or eliminating your habit of saying "good job," you might want to try getting together with colleagues for a session or workshop where you specifically focus on using substitute words for approving what children are doing.

   - First have everyone list all of the phrases of approval they can think of for telling children they approve of the *way* they did something (rather than what they did), such as those shown in Figure 34–1.

   - Go over everyone's substitute sayings. Do they express *how* children accomplished what they were supposed to do rather than *what* the accomplishment was? This encouragement helps the children rather than you to evaluate what they did, while still giving your approval.

   - Use posters or photo cards from an educational supply company such as the Good Behavior Reminder Posters from Lakeshore Learning Materials (1-800-421-5354) with your colleagues. Hold up each poster showing children practicing good behavior like sharing or brushing teeth, and ask session participants what they would say to the children to show approval and encouragement rather than praise.

2. **Look at children's art with new eyes.**

   - Finding new ways to respond to children's art without praising it can help you learn to use the same type of encouragement for children's positive behavior.

   - One class in a rural Head Start talked about the healthy foods they grew on their farms. The teacher brought in a different fruit or vegetable for snacks or lunch every day. The children then drew pictures (Figures 34–2 and 34–3) about growing healthy fruit and vegetables. What comments would you make to each of these children about their pictures if they showed them to you without their captions?

   - Just looking at their pictures, without knowing what the children had to say about them, should make a teacher respond carefully. Children see their drawings quite differently from adults. In Figure 34–2 you could say: "The bright colors of your house (red and purple with a green door) make everyone see it easily, don't you think?" or "Your garden seems to have many trees and plants." Hopefully, either of these two comments would elicit a response from the child. But as you note from the caption, the child had something else in mind.

   - In Figure 34–3 you see a child and a sun, but it is not clear about the other figures. Instead of asking the child what they are, how can you comment in a way that will encourage the child? You might say something about the large blue figure at the left: "Your blue figure is really tall." Once you hear what the child has to say about planting a seed, you may notice the orange seed at the bottom of the picture, which perhaps is growing into a horizontal orange carrot. The other figures may very well be for practice (persons? fruits?)—still a process and not a finished product.

FIGURE 34–1 "Good Job" Substitutes.

> *"Good Job" Substitutes*
>
> That was hard work.
> You really helped Brent.
> Hurray, you finished!
> How were you able to do that?
> You really showed Lisa how.
> You were quiet for ten minutes!

3. **Use "specific praise" privately to encourage children's positive behavior.**

   • Whereas *automatic* praise like saying "good job" has been shown to be ineffective (Albert, 2003), *specific* praise about an accomplishment, if given privately, does seem to motivate children and make them try harder or feel better about themselves. When children demonstrate that they can take turns, wait for a turn, express their anger in words instead of

FIGURE 34–2   "It's a Garden with Watermelons."

FIGURE 34–3   "I Planted a Seed and It Grew into a Carrot."

FIGURE 34–4 Specific
Praise for What You See.

> *Taking turns:*   "You gave Darnell a turn with the horseshoe magnet, Ross.
> Good for you!"
>
> Waiting for a turn: "You waited patiently for your turn on the computer,
> Heather."
>
> *Expressing anger in words:* "What you said to Tyler instead of hitting him
> really prevented a fight, Devin."
>
> *Helping someone:* "You helped Josh pick up the blocks without even
> being asked, Rob."

*"You gave Darnell a turn with the
horseshoe magnet, Ross. Good
for you!"*

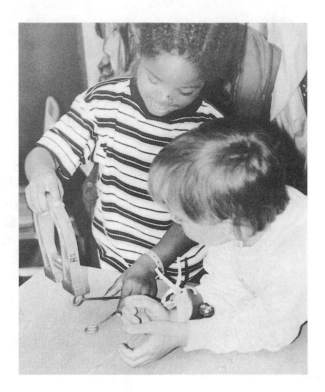

hitting, or help someone without being asked, you should definitely make a positive
comment to show that you have noticed and approve. What should you say? Specific praise
is most effective if you tell the child privately what you saw him doing. Some examples are
cited in Figure 34–4.

REFERENCES AND SUGGESTED READINGS

Albert, L. (2003). *A teacher's guide to cooperative discipline: How to manage your classroom and promote
self-esteem.* Circle Pines, MN: American Guidance Service.

Hitz, R., & Driscoll, A. (1988). Praise or encouragement? New insights into praise implications for early
childhood. *Young Children, 43*(5), 6–13.

Kohn, A. (1993). *Punished by rewards.* Boston: Houghton Mifflin.

Kohn, A. (2001). Five reasons to stop saying "Good Job!" *Young Children, 56*(5), 24–28.

Piaget, J. (1965). *Moral judgment of the child.* New York: Free Press.

Wolfgang, C. H. (2004). Teacher praise: Make informed choices. *Dimensions of Early Childhood, 32*(3), 5–10.

35

REDIRECTION

CONCEPT

Redirection is a well-known behavior strategy used by parents to divert a young child's attention away from a dangerous or off-limits situation by distracting her and getting her involved in something else. Teachers of young children can also use the same means when intervention is necessary during a conflict or other unacceptable situation. When teachers anticipate problems with certain children they can often avert them through redirection. For instance, an argument between two children that may erupt into physical aggression can sometimes be prevented by redirecting the children into different activities. When children are in conflict over an object, a teacher can sometimes substitute similar objects for the children to play with. As Marion (2003) notes:

> Substitution is a good strategy to use with older children because it acknowledges the child's desire to plan and engage in a specific activity. (p. 115)

When a child needs to calm down, he can be redirected to a calming activity as discussed in chapter 24: Materials, Calming. But when groups of children get too rambunctious milling around the classroom, the teacher may need to lead them herself into a new and exciting physical activity that will consume their energy in a positive manner. She can have her classroom ready ahead of time when it is necessary to accommodate groups of active children who may need redirection. Each child can then choose a yarn necklace to wear which tells him what activity he will pursue. Here are some examples:

STEPS

1. **Have special physical activities set up in the large motor center.**
2. **Read a book about trucks as a lead-in to special truck activities.**
3. **Have large cardboard cartons to be painted with wide brushes and constructed as emergency vehicles.**

ACTIVITIES

1. **Have special physical activities set up in the large motor center.**
   - These should be special activities brought out for times when children need redirection. Have one or two beanbag stations, for example, which you make from cardboard cartons with a target painted on the front and a hole in the middle. The energy from the milling children can thus be redirected into fun physical activities. Children can help make beanbags and targets or they can be purchased commercially (Constructive Playthings, 1-800-448-4115).
   - Have a balance board station made from a row of unit blocks or a commercial wooden balance board or curved plastic balance boards.
   - Have a frog-jump station with carpet squares that children jump from one to another on. You may want to read *One, Two, Three, JUMP!* (Lively, 1998) to motivate children to jump like frogs.

- Have a crawl-through tunnel station made from cutout cardboard cartons or commercial fabric or see-through tunnels.

2. **Read a book about trucks as a lead-in to special truck activities.**

    Trucks Whizz! Zoom! Rumble! (Hubbell, 2003)

    Dig Dig Digging (Mayo, 2002a)

    Emergency! (Mayo, 2002b)

    B Is for Bulldozer (Sobel, 2003)

    I Love Trucks! (Sturges, 1999)

- Many of the most rambunctious children may be boys, as King and Gartrell (2003) note: "Active, energetic children, notably boys, seem to spend a lot of time engaged in off-task behavior, looking for and finding mischief" (p. 33). You can redirect them to several different types of trucks and construction materials which boys especially enjoy.

- Lead your group over to the book center by telling them: "All truck drivers need to assemble in the ready room (book center) to be given their assignments for the day." After they have settled down read them one of the truck books to get them thinking and talking about what kinds of trucks there are and what they do. Then give out the "assignments" (numbered yarn necklaces).

- Number one's can be given a set of Lego Systems Vehicles (Constructive Playthings) and blocks to work with at one of the tables. Number two's can be given a box of small digging trucks (bulldozer, crane, front loader, dump truck, etc.) along with safety goggles to be used at the sand table. Number three's can be given trucks to be used on the floor in the block center. Let them choose their numbers and give them time to play out their scenarios. They may want to exchange necklaces when they are finished and play in the other areas if time permits.

3. **Have large cardboard cartons to be painted with wide brushes and constructed as emergency vehicles.**

- Have two children work on each box and ask them what kind of vehicle they would like to construct. Read the book *Emergency!* (Mayo, 2002b) to give them some examples. Put newspapers on the floor and give them brushes and paint to paint their vehicles. Then they can paint paper plates to attach as wheels, headlights, and a steering wheel. Afterwards encourage them to enact emergency vehicle scenarios.

Some children can choose trucks to be used on the floor in the block center.

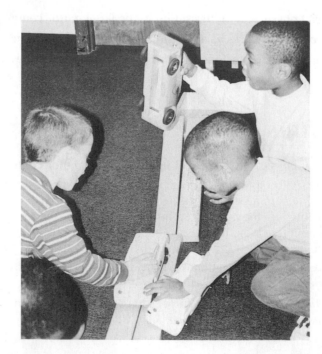

REFERENCES AND SUGGESTED READINGS

Beaty, J. J. (1999). *Prosocial guidance for the preschool child.* Upper Saddle River, NJ: Merrill/Prentice Hall.

King, M., & Gartrell, D. (2003). Building an encouraging classroom with boys in mind. *Young Children, 58*(4), 33–36.

Marion, M. (2003). *Guidance of young children* (6th ed.). Upper Saddle River, NJ: Merrill/Prentice Hall.

Children's Books

Hubbell, P. (2003). *Trucks whizz! Zoom! Rumble!* New York: Marshall Canvendish.

Lively, L. (1998). *One, two, three, JUMP!* New York: Simon & Schuster.

Mayo, M. (2002a). *Dig dig digging.* New York: Henry Holt & Company, Inc.

Mayo, M. (2002b). *Emergency!* Minneapolis, MN: Carolrhoda Books, Inc.*

Sobel, J. (2003). *B is for bulldozer.* San Diego: Harcourt, Inc.

Sturges, P. (1999). *I love trucks!* New York: HarperCollins.

---

*multicultural

36 REINFORCEMENT

CONCEPT

Reinforcement has long been a positive guidance strategy for teachers of young children. Wolfgang (2004) describes it as:

> Reinforcement is a behavioral principle that describes a direct relationship between two real events: a behavior (an observable action, such as staying seated during story time), and a consequence (as a result of the act, the child gets a treat at the end of the story). (p. 8)

Teachers do give positive reinforcement to children who display appropriate behavior but generally not in the form of a treat. Treats, stickers, stars, and prizes are known as "tangible reinforcers." More frequently teachers use "social reinforcers" such as smiles, nods, winks, hand signs, and specific praise, or sometimes "activity reinforcers" such as playing with special toys. Positive reinforcement should act as an inducement for a child to continue the appropriate behavior, but it needs to be repeated many times for real learning to take place. Every time the rambunctious child plays without hitting or pushing, the teacher needs to show she approves with a smile or nod, or specific praise such as, "You played with the boys really peacefully this morning, Luis."

For the teacher, positive reinforcement helps her focus on a child's desirable behavior and try to ignore the inappropriate behavior. Too frequently teachers focus on children's inappropriate behavior—hitting, pushing, yelling, taking things—because it is so attention-getting. It seems to call out for the teacher to stop it. The disruptive child, in fact, may be calling out for adult attention even if it means punishment. A teacher's response can stop the behavior temporarily, but it also reinforces it in a negative way. It leads the child to believe: "If I behave this way, the teacher will notice me." If you must intervene to stop this behavior, do it as quickly and unobtrusively as possible without making eye contact with the child. Later when the child has calmed down you can positively reinforce the child with smiles and specific praise.

But if you find yourself rushing to stop an unruly child with loud verbal commands and know you need to break this habitual behavior, what can you do? It may not be easy to shift your attention to the positive and ignore the child's disruptive behavior. It calls for the changing of a mind-set and a definite action to bring about a change in yourself before you can expect a change in a child.

STEPS

1. **Make a list of positive behaviors a disruptive child displays for a day.**
2. **Each time the child displays a positive behavior reinforce it with a smile, a nod, or a word of encouragement; ignore disruptive behavior.**
3. **If the behavior involves harm to another child or damage to materials, remove the child or material without speaking or making eye contact.**
4. **As soon as the child displays desirable behavior go to her immediately and express your pleasure.**

ACTIVITIES

1. **Make a list of positive behaviors a disruptive child displays for a day.**
   - Share what you are doing with the other staff members. They can add to your list or make one of their own. Keep a pad and pencil on top of the room dividers so you can catch the child's behavior in every learning center. You may find yourself wanting to write down disruptive behaviors, as well, but restrain yourself. Figure 36–1 is a sample list for the first two hours.

2. **Each time the child displays a positive behavior reinforce it with a smile, a nod, or a word of encouragement; ignore disruptive behavior.**
   - The teacher's responses are shown on the right side of Figure 36–1. Shandra noticed that the teacher was observing her and writing. She tried several disruptive actions but the teacher turned her head and did not respond again until she saw Shandra displaying a positive behavior. Some of the unrecorded disruptive behaviors included: interrupting different children in the learning centers by pushing materials around and knocking things on the floor. When the teacher mentioned "What a tall tower!" she knocked it down. She picked up as many plastic fruits as she could hold and went around the room dropping them here and there. When that did not draw the teacher's response, she finally put the plastic bananas back in a pan.
   - The teacher talked with the staff about this experience. They decided to try it for several days with other staff members observing and recording to see if Shandra would understand that the only way she could draw their attention was by leaving other children's things alone and playing with her materials at a table. Other staff members also had trouble not recording Shandra's interruptions, but by the third day she interrupted only twice. Teachers and the child were all learning about positive reinforcement.

Hangs coat in cubby	Waves, says, "Hi, Shandra."
Talks briefly with Karen	Smiles, nods
Walks in room carefully	Smiles
Sits in morning circle briefly	Makes eye contact, smiles
Walks around looking at activities	Says, "Here's a neat puzzle."
Stops and talks to Karen again	Smiles
Stands and watches Karen paint	Says, "You know how to do that, too."
Shakes head "no" when teacher asks her about painting	"Want to paint?"
Sits down at table and stacks blocks	"What a tall tower!"
Tells teacher she's hungry	"Okay, snacks are ready."
Eats snack hurriedly	"You've got a good appetite."
Rushes over to play corner	Smiles
Picks up plastic fruits	"Want to play with Cassy?"
Walks around holding fruits	No comment
Puts banana in pan	"Thanks for knowing where to put the bananas."

FIGURE 36–1 Shandra's Positive Behaviors; Teacher's Responses.

Shandra puts the bananas back in the pan.

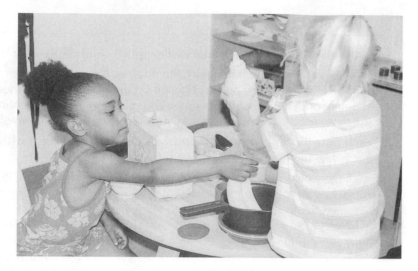

3. **If the behavior involves harm to another child or damage to materials, remove the child or material without speaking or making eye contact.**
   - This happened only once with Shandra. When she knocked the little suitcase off the table and across the floor, the teacher quickly picked it up and put it away without looking at Shandra or saying a word. After that Shandra played normally with materials, often looking around to see if a teacher was watching.

4. **As soon as the child displays desirable behavior go to her immediately and express your pleasure.**
   - The teacher who picked up the suitcase that Shandra had knocked off the table put it away and waited until she saw the girl playing normally with the other materials on the table. Then she went over and commented: "You certainly know how to cook a pretend meal, Shandra."

REFERENCES AND SUGGESTED READINGS

Adams, S. K., & Baronberg, J. (2005). *Promoting positive behaviors: Guidance strategies for early childhood settings.* Upper Saddle River, NJ: Merrill/Prentice Hall.

Beaty, J. J. (2004). *Skills for preschool teachers* (7th ed.). Upper Saddle River, NJ: Merrill/Prentice Hall.

Duncan, T. K., Kemple, K. M., & Smith, T. M. (2000). Reinforcement in developmentally appropriate early childhood classrooms. *Childhood Education, 76,* 194–203.

Wolfgang, C. H. (2000/01). Another view on "Reinforcement in developmentally appropriate early childhood classrooms." *Childhood Education, 77*(2), 64–67.

Wolfgang, C. H. (2004). Teacher praise: Make informed choices. *Dimensions of Early Childhood, 32*(3), 5–10.

37

RULE-MAKING

CONCEPT

Young children know about rules. They have had to live by rules in most families. They are used to being reminded to follow the rules. But this does not mean they like rules or even understand them. Because most rules are made by the adults around them, they more or less accept them without much thought. Sometimes they follow them, sometimes they don't. But what would happen if the children themselves were involved in rule-making? Teachers who have involved children in making classroom rules often find that when children know what is expected of them they are better behaved and more cooperative in following the rules. On the other hand, teachers who have not included children in the rule-making process have some concerns, as pointed out by DeVries and Zan (1994):

> Many teachers feel nervous at first about turning the rule-making process over to children. They may believe children cannot make rules. They may fear that children will make unacceptable rules, or worse yet, no rules at all. These fears have not been realized in our experience of observing young children participate in rule making. (p. 126)

On the contrary, children who help develop classroom rules begin to understand what rules are about and why they are necessary. They also feel an ownership in classroom decisions as well as a responsibility for what happens in the classroom. How can a teacher go about involving the children in developing the classroom rules?

STEPS

1. **Develop the rules at the beginning of the year.**
2. **Help children learn to apply the rules when the occasion arises.**
3. **Use puppets to model the rules.**
4. **Read picture books to illustrate the rules.**

ACTIVITIES

1. **Develop the rules at the beginning of the year.**
   - One teacher always starts the year by calling the children together for a meeting on how to make the classroom a peaceful place for everyone. She wants the rules they decide on to be for the benefit of the children and not just for herself. Although she directs the discussion, she allows the children free rein to talk about their wants and needs.
   - The amount of noise is always one concern, as is the amount of running around and pushing. When it gets too loud children cannot hear one another, let alone the teacher. The teacher

Room 2's Rules.

makes a list of their concerns, then with their help converts these concerns into simple rules. She understands that the rules they all agree on must be:

Few in number

Very brief

Easy to understand

Positive, not negative in their wording

An example of the rules this classroom agreed on is shown in the photograph above. Making simple drawings beside each rule to illustrate it helps these nonliterate children to understand the rule and even begin to read it.

Walking feet

Inside voices

Listening ears

Keep your hands to yourself

2. **Help children learn to apply the rules when the occasion arises.**
    - Children come to understand rules by seeing them in action. For instance, when children actually start running around they can be reminded about "walking feet." Who does the reminding? Both teacher and children. At first it is the teacher who points out their rule on the rule poster, and has someone demonstrate what it means. Eventually children themselves remind runners to use "walking feet" in the classroom.
    - When the classroom gets too noisy someone (teacher or child) will whisper very loudly: "Inside voices," and put a finger up to his mouth. Or when the teacher wants the room quiet enough to hear someone speak, she may say: "Listening ears," and point to her ears.
    - When children roughhouse, push, or hit one another the teacher will tap the children involved on the shoulder and, without a word, will point to the sign: "Keep your hands to yourself." Or sometimes she will take a forgetful child's hands and put them down on his sides, then nod to the sign.

3. **Use puppets to model the rules.**
    - Using puppets to illustrate rules is always an effective way to get a point across. This is not a puppet show, but the teacher putting one puppet on her hand and offering a second puppet to another child. Her puppet is always "Dollmer-don't-know-how." She asks a small group of

children: "Who would like to teach Dollmer how to walk in the classroom?" The child who puts the second puppet on her hand can give her puppet a name if she wants. Then the teacher makes Dollmer stomp heavily across an imaginary room. The child's puppet must tell or show Dollmer the correct way to walk. He can try skipping, hopping, or running while the child keeps after him with her puppet until he finally learns the right way, and everyone claps. This kind of learning is not only fun for the children, but very effective.

• Dollmer can also shout, push, or hit others in funny ways at various times, while another child uses a second puppet to try to remind him of the rules. If children really understand Dollmer's role and would like to play Dollmer themselves, turn both puppets over to the children. But afterward put the puppets away until another rule-teaching occasion arises.

4. **Read picture books to illustrate the rules.**

• Read each of the following books to one or two children or to one small group at a time so that listeners can see the illustrations clearly and can help to decide what rules should apply (if any) to the situation, and how the characters can learn the rules.

• In *Trouble in the Barkers' Class* (dePaola, 2003) a new student comes to school and breaks all the rules, making it very uncomfortable for the rest of the students. As you read the story, ask your listeners to think about what they would do. Stop before the end of the story and ask what they decided. Then read how the students resolved the problem.

• In *Hunter's Best Friend in School* (Elliott, 2002) Stripe makes all sorts of mischief in school, getting Hunter involved, too. Were any rules broken? What does their teacher do? How would your listeners solve this problem? How does Hunter solve it?

• In *Tissue, Please!* (Kopelke, 2004) Frog and his friends in his ballet class all have the sniffles. Their teacher gets very upset. Their performance is almost ruined. Were any rules broken? How was the problem solved?

• In *Too Loud Lily* (Laguna, 2002), everything Lily Hippo does is too loud: her talking, her singing, even her yawning. She gets sent to the principal's office. What rules were broken? How was her problem solved?

• In *No, David!* (Shannon, 1998) David's mother tries to prevent David from making mischief in the house by saying "no." Does it work? What does she finally do?

REFERENCES AND SUGGESTED READINGS

Adams, S. K., & Baronberg, J. (2005). *Promoting positive behavior: Guidance strategies for early childhood settings.* Upper Saddle River, NJ: Merrill/Prentice Hall.
Beaty, J. J. (1999). *Prosocial guidance for the preschool child.* Upper Saddle River, NJ: Merrill/Prentice Hall.
DeVries, R., & Zan, B. (1994). *Moral classrooms, moral children: Creating a constructivist atmosphere in early education.* New York: Teachers College Press.
Howes, C., & Ritchie, S. (2002). *A matter of trust: Connecting teachers and learners in the early childhood classroom.* New York: Teachers College Press.
Levin, D. E. (2003). *Teaching young children in violent times: Building a peaceable classroom* (2nd ed.). Washington, DC: National Association for the Education of Young Children.
Rightmyer, E. C. (2003). Democratic discipline: Children creating solutions. *Young Children, 58*(4), 38–45.

Children's Books
dePaola, T. (2003). *Trouble in the Barkers' class.* New York: G. P. Putnam's Sons.
Elliott, L. M. (2002). *Hunter's best friend in school.* New York: HarperCollins.
Kopelke, L. (2004). *Tissue, please!* New York: Simon & Schuster.
Laguna, S. (2002). *Too loud Lily.* New York: Scholastic Press.
Shannon, D. (1998). *No, David!* New York: The Blue Sky Press.

38 SELF-ESTEEM

CONCEPT

The concept that young children need to have positive esteem themselves has long been a guiding principle in early childhood programs. Children who do not feel good about themselves are often the ones who disrupt the classroom or withdraw into apathy. If we can change their perception to a positive one, will it also change their behavior? Many teachers believe it will.

Young children's feelings about themselves develop over time as they interact with the people around them. Self-esteem—*an individual's evaluation of himself*—may not emerge fully until middle childhood (Harter, 1998), but the development begins in infancy as relationships evolve between children and their parents and later between children and their teachers. How parents and teachers treat young children and what they expect of them help to color children's feelings about themselves. DeVries and Zan (1994) believe that low self-esteem often results:

> When the child experiences adults as predominantly controlling, the self that is constructed is an indecisive one that needs or seeks control by others. (p. 48)

On the other hand, when adults refrain from exercising unnecessary authority they open the way for children to regulate their behavior voluntarily, a relationship Piaget (1954/1981) calls *autonomous* or *cooperative,* in which children often exhibit high self-esteem. Thus, the way you interact with the children in your classroom can have an important effect on the way they feel about themselves. How will you know how they feel? Observing children using an observational checklist may be helpful. Figure 38–1 lists seven items that children with high self-esteem often exhibit.

Teachers, student interns, and volunteers can take turns observing all the children one-by-one until they have compiled a list of children who may need help strengthening their self-esteem. Then they can decide how to interact with these children using the following steps:

FIGURE 38–1 Self-Esteem Checklist.

> _____ Develops secure attachment relationship with teacher
>
> _____ Makes activity choices without teacher's help
>
> _____ Seeks other children to play with
>
> _____ Will join in play with other children
>
> _____ Shows pride in accomplishments
>
> _____ Moves with confidence
>
> _____ Can do things independently

STEPS

1. **Let child know she/he is accepted.**
2. **Help children to accept themselves.**
3. **Help children to experience success.**

ACTIVITIES

1. **Let child know she/he is accepted.**
   - Teachers and other team members need to welcome each child individually every day with a warm smile and a sincere greeting such as: "I'm so glad to see you this morning," or "I missed you yesterday. Welcome back!"
   - Teachers need to circulate around the room for a private word or two with each child during the free-choice period when children are busily engaged in the various learning centers. They can ask her about her project, exclaim about his block building, or talk about favorite colors and foods.
   - Be sure to ask each child in turn to help you with some special task such as mixing paints, getting out cots, delivering a note to the room next door, or looking for a missing puzzle piece. Children need to feel wanted like this. Keep track of which children you ask, so that no one will be left out.
2. **Help children to accept themselves.**
   - Involve the children in self-esteem art activities (see Figure 38–2) that will help them use painting, play dough, hand stamping, or footprint making to be displayed on the wall or in a class scrapbook.
   - Read self-esteem picture books like those listed in Figure 38–3 to individuals and small groups. Can they pretend they are the book characters telling everyone what they feel about themselves?
   - After hearing some of these books your children should be able to tell you what is beautiful about them, too.

Teachers need to talk with each child during the free-choice period about something of interest to the child.

FIGURE 38–2 When the Teacher Asked the Children to Draw Pictures of Themselves Showing How Good Food Made Them Feel, This Girl Drew a Big Smile and Muscles.

FIGURE 38–3 Books with Self-Esteem Theme.

> *Incredible Me!* (Appelt, 2003)*
>
> *What Is Beautiful?* (Avery, 1995)*
>
> *I Can Do It Too!* (Baicker, 2003)*
>
> *I Like Myself* (Beaumont, 2004)*
>
> *I'm Gonna Like Me: Letting Off a Little Self-Esteem* (Curtis, 2002)
>
> *I Am Me* (Kustin, 2000)*
>
> *Stand Tall, Molly Lou Melon* (Lovell, 2001)*

*multicultural

3. **Help children to experience success.**

   - What can children do on their own in your classroom? Being successful in an activity makes children feel really good about themselves. The following is a list of items many children are able to accomplish. When any of your children achieve any of these be sure to mention it or congratulate them.

   ### Children's Independent Skills

Putting on jacket	Putting on paint apron	Toileting
Zipping jacket	Helping make play dough	Washing hands
Tying shoes	Painting with brush	Brushing teeth
Operating computer	Making a puzzle	Cleaning up after eating
Operating tape recorder	Singing a song	Sliding down slide
Pounding in nails	Building a building	Climbing across bars
Cutting with scissors	Putting blocks away	Riding trike, scooter
Following recipe chart	Setting table for eating	Throwing, catching
Writing own name	Dishing out own food	Jumping rope
Returning borrowed book	Pouring own drink	Making swing go

As Kosnik (1993) points out:

> *For children to believe that they are valuable members of the community, they must feel individually noticed and they must feel wanted. By getting to know the children and highlighting their abilities, the teacher validates the children. She is one step closer to increasing the children's self-esteem. (p. 36)*

REFERENCES AND SUGGESTED READINGS

Ariza-Evans, M. (2004). Self-esteem and young children: Guiding principles. *Dimensions of Early Childhood, 32*(1), 21–27.

DeVries, R., & Zan, B. (1994). *Moral classrooms, moral children: Creating a constructivist atmosphere in early education.* New York: Teachers College Press.

Ferber, J. (1996). A look in the mirror: Self-concept in preschool children. In L. Koplow (Ed.), *Unsmiling faces: How preschools can heal.* New York: Teachers College Press.

Harter, S. (1998). The development of self-representation. In W. Damon & N. Eisenberg (Eds.), *Handbook of child psychology: Social, emotional, and personality development.* New York: Wiley.

Kosnick, C. (1993). Everyone is a V.I.P. in this class. *Young Children, 49*(1), 32–37.

Marshall, H. H. (2001). Cultural influences on the development of self-concept: Updating our thinking. *Young Children, 56*(6), 19–25.

Piaget, J. (1954/1981). *Intelligence and affectivity: Their relation during child development.* Palo Alto, CA: Annual Reviews.

Wardle, F. (1995). How young children build images of themselves. *Child Care Information Exchange, 7,* 44–47.

Children's Books

Appelt, K. (2003). *Incredible me!* New York: HarperCollins.*

Avery, M. W. (1995). *What is beautiful?* Berkeley, CA: Tricycle Press.*

Baicker, K. (2003). *I can do it too!* Brooklyn, NY: Handprint Books.*

Beaumont, K. (2004). *I like myself.* Orlando, FL: Harcourt, Inc.*

Curtis, J. L. (2002). *I'm gonna like me: Letting off a little self-esteem.* New York: Joanna Cottler Books.

Kuskin, K. (2000). *I am me.* New York: Simon & Schuster.*

Lovell, P. (2001). *Stand tall, Molly Lou Melon.* New York: G. P. Putnam's Sons.*

———

*multicultural

39 SELF-REGULATION

CONCEPT

As young children become more familiar with the classroom schedule, the activities available, and their own needs and interests, most of them want to exercise as much independence as possible in how they spend their time. The "self-regulation" referred to in this strategy concerns the methods children can use for participating in classroom learning centers or using materials on their own without teacher direction.

Children need opportunities to make meaningful choices as well as assistance in developing strategies for becoming independent in learning activities. As Bronson (2000) points out:

> Children learn self-regulatory skills in a responsive social and material environment that provides opportunities for effective action and is predictable enough to allow children to recognize the effects of their efforts. (p. 36)

Most early childhood classooms offer a wide variety of learning centers that children can choose to use: blocks, books, dramatic play, music, art, manipulatives, science, math, sand and water play, writing, computer, woodworking, and large motor activities. The problem has always been: How many children can use each of these centers at a time? Does the teacher have to be the one to tell them? Can those who get to a favorite center first keep others out? When a center is full, does the teacher have to tell others to find another activity? The strategy of self-regulation discussed here can help resolve these problems.

As Bronson points out, Vygotsky (1962, 1978) considered language the primary means for developing both understanding and self-regulation. "The child internalizes the instructions given by others and begins to give herself audible directions" (p. 34). We believe that young children can also teach themselves to regulate themselves through the use of self-regulating devices.

STEPS

1. **Give children opportunities to make meaningful choices among learning activities.**
2. **Show children how to use self-regulating devices to carry out independent learning activities.**

ACTIVITIES

1. **Give children opportunities to make meaningful choices among learning activities.**

   - First, children need to recognize what activities are available for independent learning choices. If you have arranged the classroom with learning centers clearly delineated and labeled, children can see what is available during the free-choice period. Materials in the centers should be neatly arranged on the shelves with appropriate labels or placed on tables ready for children's use. Goggles for sand play and woodworking should be hanging near the tables. Painting aprons should be ready for use.

   - New materials can be introduced to everyone and turn-taking arrangements agreed upon.

FIGURE 39–1 Self-Regulating Devices.

- Learning center necklaces or tags
- Tickets for popular activities or toys
- Drawing names or numbers out of a hat
- Sign-up sheets or clipboards
- Kitchen timers or egg hourglasses

2. **Show children how to use self-regulating devices to carry out independent learning activities.**

- Teachers and children together can devise a variety of self-regulating devices that children choose and use when they are in the various learning centers. These are usually discussed and agreed upon ahead of time by the children and teachers, and provided by the teachers soon afterward. Figure 39–1 lists some of the self-regulating devices used.

- Learning center necklaces tend to be very popular these days. They are necklaces made of yarn with the name or sign of the center attached to them, to be hung on hooks at the front of the center. The number of hooks and necklaces denote the number of children who can be in the center at one time.

- When children leave the center they rehang their necklace on its hook. Or they may trade their necklace with someone from another learning center. Some children prefer to use name tags or picture tags to hang on an empty hook in a center. The number of hooks or tags always tells the number of children that can occupy a center at one time. If children note there are more children in a center than should be there, they will tell others to wait until a necklace or tag is free.

REFERENCES AND SUGGESTED READINGS

Beaty, J. J. (2004). *Skills for preschool teachers.* Upper Saddle River, NJ: Merrill/Prentice Hall.

Bronson, M. B. (2000). Recognizing and supporting the development of self-regulation in young children. *Young Children, 55*(2), 32–37.

Vygotsky, L. (1962). *Thought and language.* Cambridge, MA: MIT Press.

Vygotsky, L. (1978). *Mind in society: The development of higher psychological processes.* Cambridge, MA: Harvard University Press.

This girl is hanging her name tag in the fine arts center.

40 SHARING

CONCEPT

Sharing is one of the most difficult concepts for young children to learn. Why should they give something of theirs to someone else? Why should they divide up the candy or let someone else play with one of their favorite trucks? There is something about personal ownership that makes it difficult for young children to part with anything they have a claim on, be it clothes, candy, or toys. In an early childhood classroom they must learn new ways of behavior or forever be engaged in conflicts with the others around them.

When children first enter the classroom is the time to begin dealing with this issue. Many children are all but overwhelmed with the number of toys and activities available—all for them, they may believe at first. Many are used to having a set of their own playthings at home, and assume that the same rules apply here. But because everything is different in this new environment, perhaps the rules are, too. Most young children are good at adapting to new and different situations. Thus it is up to the teachers and staff members to set the positive tone at the outset that we all need to share the toys and materials that belong to the classroom—children and teachers alike—and then demonstrate how it is done. Sharing is dividing up or giving something you have possession of to someone else. Marion (2003) notes that:

> Sharing seems to serve another important purpose for young children in social interactions. Offering things to others—often viewed as sharing—is one way that a young child can initiate social contact and then keep the interaction going once it has started. (p. 302)

STEPS

1. **Read books about sharing and talk about them.**
2. **Acknowledge and thank children who share.**
3. **Have materials for two to share.**
4. **Have a sharing toy that all must share.**

ACTIVITIES

1. **Read books about sharing and talk about them.**
   - Children may not really understand what sharing is all about. Reading books to individuals and small groups can help them learn about this prosocial skill when they see book characters practicing it. In *Will I Have a Friend?* (Cohen, 1967) Jim is worried about finding a friend on the first day of nursery school until finally Paul reaches out and shares his little truck with him. Ask your listeners what other sharing could have happened in that class.
   - In *Building a Bridge* (Begaye, 1993) Juanita, a Navajo girl, and Anna, an Anglo girl, are nervous on their first day of kindergarten until Juanita finds a bucket of purple and green blocks they can share. At first Anna builds a green bridge and Juanita a purple one, but then

they decide to put their blocks together to build a much larger bridge. Sharing all the blocks finally brings them together because it doesn't matter what color the blocks are.

- In *Jamaica Tag-Along* (Havill, 1989) Jamaica's older brother tells her not to tag-along when she interrupts his basketball game with the bigger boys in the park. So she decides to build a castle in the sand pile, but little Berto keeps interrupting her. Finally she realizes she is acting toward him just like her brother did toward her, so she shares building the castle with him. Can your listeners tell you how this sharing is different from Jim's and Paul's?

- In *Just Not the Same* (Lacoe, 1992) Cleo, Mirabelle, and Gertrude are sisters who will not share anything. Their mother cuts an apple for them into three pieces but they argue over whose is the largest, so their mother takes and makes it into applesauce. The same thing happens with riding in the car and sleeping in bunk beds. Finally they have to share when they get one puppy.

2. **Acknowledge and thank children who share.**

- Keep your eyes open for children who share and be sure to acknowledge and thank them for it. Make a fuss about it, saying that's what it takes for everyone to get along in this world. When you see children sharing, try to determine who initiates it: the child who shares, a friend who asks for the toy, or an adult who tells the child to let someone else have a turn. As Eisenberg (1992) notes:

   In the preschool classroom, much of children's prosocial behavior is directed toward the few children with whom they play most, and children tend to share with and help those children who share with and help them. (p. 15)

- Have a labeled Sharing Jar on a shelf in a prominent place in the classroom. Write down on a slip of paper the name of each child every time she shares and let her put it in the jar. As noted by Adams and Baronberg (2005), "Even under the best of circumstances, children need time and practice to become good at prosocial behaviors" (p. 67). Use different color paper slips for every month, so children can see this is something that is ongoing. Hopefully there will be an increase of the present month's color slips as children make a practice of sharing.

3. **Have materials for two to share.**

- Now that children understand a bit about sharing, let them try it out. Set up one glob of play dough on a table with two chairs for two to share. Do they divide it up and play separately or play with it together?

- Put one glob of finger paint on a table with two chairs and one sheet of paper and see what happens. Do the children play with it together? Can they get along? Be sure to acknowledge their sharing if they do any.

- Put a jar with three crayons on a table with two chairs and one sheet of paper and watch how they use the crayons. Don't forget to acknowledge sharing.

4. **Have a sharing toy that all must share.**

- Bring in a large stuffed giraffe and read the book *Giraffes Can't Dance* (Andreae, 1999). Tell the children who want to play with Gerald the Giraffe that they will have to work out a way to share him. Watch and see what happens.

- Bring in a large red fire truck and fire fighter figures. Children who want to play with the truck and figures will have to share them. Some may want to use the "self-regulation devices" they previously learned about. Make up other similar sharing activities from time to time.

REFERENCES AND SUGGESTED READINGS

Adams, S. K., & Baronberg, J. (2005). *Promoting positive behavior.* Upper Saddle River, NJ: Merrill/Prentice Hall.

Cartledge, G., & Milburn, J. F. (1995). *Teaching social skills to children and youth: Innovative approaches* (3rd ed.). Boston: Allyn & Bacon.

Eisenberg, N. (1992). *The caring child.* Cambridge, MA: Harvard University Press.

Marion, M. (2003). *Guidance of young children.* Upper Saddle River, NJ: Merrill/Prentice Hall.

Miller, S. (2000). Sharing. *Scholastic Early Childhood Today, 25*(2), 32–33.

Poole, C., Miller, S., & Church, E. B. (1998). Share with me! *Scholastic Early Childhood Today, 18*(3), 18–21.

Children's Books

Andreae, G. (1999). *Giraffes can't dance.* New York: Orchard.

Begaye, L. S. (1993). *Building a bridge.* Flagstaff, AZ: Northland.*

Cohen, M. (1967). *Will I have a friend?* New York: Collier Books.*

Havill, J. (1989). *Jamaica Tag-Along.* Boston: Houghton Mifflin.*

Lacoe, A. (1992). *Just not the same.* Boston: Houghton Mifflin.

———————

*multicultural

41

STORMS

CONCEPT

When warnings for violent weather such as tornadoes, tropical storms, hurricanes, typhoons, electrical storms, hail storms, windstorms, dust storms, or blizzards are issued, teachers need to be prepared ahead of time to provide both physical and psychological protection for their children. Different rules apply to the different types of storms. You need to learn the rules that apply in your particular area and practice them with the children until they can respond quickly and without panic. If evacuation is necessary read chapter 10: Emergencies for advice on what to do.

In electrical storms children need to come inside as quickly as possible. If they get caught outside, they should not stand under trees or stay in water. They may need to wait out the storm in a vehicle. Inside the classroom, computers should be unplugged and telephones disconnected. In tornadoes children should go to the lowest location in the building or lie down next to an inside wall in a hallway away from windows. In tropical storms, hurricanes, and typhoons children should already have been evacuated to an emergency shelter by their families.

Overcoming children's fears during violent storms is a major psychological concern for the classroom teacher. Helping children gain self-control in panic-causing situations is also a safety factor. But as Simpson and McGuire (2004) tell us:

> There is no single best way for adults to best cope with unexpected trauma or its aftermath, but there are ways to provide children with the support they need to deal with their feelings and their fears. (p. 35)

Some of the following steps may help.

STEPS

1. **Follow the strategies in Figure 41–1 to help children lessen fears.**
2. **Read storm-related stories both during and after the storm.**
3. **Be alert for aftereffects of storm-related trauma and help children return to normal.**

FIGURE 41–1 Strategies for Helping Children Lessen Fears.

1. Reduce the cause of fear wherever possible.
2. Give support and comfort to the children.
3. Allow children to cry.
4 Redirect children's attention to calming activities.
5. Help children to verbalize feelings.
6. Involve children in helping others.
7. Model controlled behavior yourself.

Note: Adapted from *Safety in Preschool Programs* (p. 16) by J. J. Beaty, 2004. Upper Saddle River, NJ: Merrill/Prentice Hall.

ACTIVITIES

1. Follow the strategies in Figure 41–1 to help children lessen fears.

- If children exhibit fear of a violent thunderstorm with lightning flashing and thunder rolling, you can close the window curtains or blinds and gather the children together in a group, perhaps in a circle on the floor where you can sing songs together, tell a funny story, or play a game like "Pass the Shoe."

- Pass the shoe quickly around the circle, while you sing the song or say the words: "Pass the shoe from me to you, to you. Pass the shoe and do just as I do." Whoever ends up with the shoe needs to copy the funny movement you make. Then start the shoe around again. Engaging the children in games like this should distract them from the fear-producing storm outside.

- Be prepared with several battery-operated lamps or lanterns for the lights to go off. If they do, just go on with whatever you are doing and turn your lanterns on. Can the children pretend they are camping out?

- Have staff members comfort crying children when necessary as you work with the total group. They can hold or rock such children or whisper funny words to them. If children want to talk about their feelings, encourage this.

- Have one of the more secure children play with anyone who seems quite distressed. This is the time to get out a box of "secret toys" (i.e., little emergency vehicles or people figures you have been saving for such an occasion).

- Use some of the calming activities described in chapter 24: Materials, Calming. Be sure you yourself exhibit calming behavior.

2. Read storm-related stories both during and after the storm.

Thunder Cake (Polacco, 1990)

Aunt Minnie and the Twister (Prigger, 2002)

Storm in the Night (Stolz, 1988)*

Storm Is Coming! (Tekavec, 2002)

Hurricane (Wiesner, 1990)

*multicultural

- Any of these books should hold the children's attention because the book characters are able to overcome any fears they may have. In *Thunder Cake* the little girl's grandma involves her in making a cake in the midst of the storm. You could have your children hull strawberries for dipping in a cream cheese dip and call them "thunder berries."

- After the twister Aunt Minnie's nine nieces and nephews find their little farm house turned completely around and they have to build a new front room. After the hurricane, the two boys find a giant tree has fallen in their yard. So they pretend is it an African jungle with elephants and leopards, a pirate ship on the seven seas, and a rocket ship that carries them to a new planet. What do your children find outside after the storm is over?

3. Be alert for aftereffects of storm-related trauma and help children return to normal.

- When children have experienced a violent storm where damage has been done, teachers need to be alert for aftereffects. As Alat (2002) points out:

   After a traumatic event, such as an earthquake, children may believe that the disaster will happen again, or they may even feel that they are responsible for the disaster. (p. 3)

- It is important for you to encourage all the children to talk about the event and for you to listen closely to what they have to say. Even weeks afterward, the event may still be on their minds. Watch children as they play to see if any signs of anxiety and tension can be detected. Talk to them privately or with a puppet on your hand. They can whisper their feelings to the puppet if they are shy about expressing them aloud. Help them to clarify what happened.

FIGURE 41–2 A Cow, My House, Storm Clouds, Rain, and the Cow's House.

- Some children may want to tell a story about what happened at their house. Others may want to paint or draw the story of the event. Even if their words do not express strong feelings, such feelings are often released through art (see Figure 41–2).

REFERENCES AND SUGGESTED READINGS

Alat, K. (2002). Traumatic events and children: How early childhood educators can help. *Childhood Education, 79*(1), 2–8.

Beaty, J. J. (2004). *Safety in preschool programs.* Upper Saddle River, NJ: Merrill/Prentice Hall.

Farish, J. M. (2001). Helping young children in frightening times. *Young Children, 56*(6), 6–7.

Oehlberg, B. (1996). *Making it better: Activities for children living in a stressful world.* St. Paul, MN: Redleaf Press.

Simpson, C. G., & McGuire, M. (2004). Are you ready? Supporting children in an uncertain world. *Dimensions of Early Childhood, 32*(3), 35–38.

Winter, R. E., Surr, J. V., & Leaf, B. J. (2003). Meeting child care needs in disasters. *Young Children, 58*(4), 82–84.

Children's Books

Polacco, P. (1990). *Thunder cake.* New York: Philomel Books.

Prigger, M. S. (2002). *Aunt Minnie and the twister.* New York: Clarion Books.

Stolz, M. (1988). *Storm in the night.* New York: HarperCollins.*

Tekavec, H. (2002). *Storm is coming.* New York: Dial Books.

Wiesner, D. (1990). *Hurricane.* New York: Clarion Books.

———
*multicultural

42 STRESS

CONCEPT

Information from brain research is helping teachers of young children understand a great deal more about how children behave and learn. For example, findings on how the brain works show that high levels of stress can inhibit learning and functioning. Webster's (1999) defines *stress* as a "physical, mental, or emotional strain or tension" (p. 1293). How does the brain respond to stress? Children assimilate large amounts of information about what is going on around them through their senses. These sensory stimuli are relayed to the brain through the firing of the nerve cells' dentrites. This information is then passed on to the various parts of the brain that control appropriate responses. If the information is threatening, children may freeze up and be unable to function normally. Or they may act in an out-of-control manner (Ruston, 2001).

It is obvious that the early childhood classroom must provide a stress-free environment in order for children to function effectively. What are some of the causes of stress in the classroom that teachers can correct? Figure 42–1 lists some.

STEPS

1. **Involve children in activities because they find them fun to do.**
2. **Show respect for and acceptance of children through your communication.**
3. **Express delight and humor around children.**
4. **Soundproof the room.**

ACTIVITIES

1. **Involve children in activities because they find them fun to do.**

   - There is never a need to threaten a child or group of children in an early childhood program. If teachers want children to do something they may not want to do, teachers should approach the situation in a fun, exciting manner, just as children love to do. For example, picking up hundreds of blocks strewn all over the floor may be a chore that seems overwhelming to all concerned. Children who emptied the shelves may quickly scatter to the far corners of the room if they think the teacher will try to force them to pick up by using a threat such as: "You

FIGURE 42–1 Causes of Stress in the Classroom.

- Teacher using threats or ridicule
- Teacher communicating with restrictive language
- Teacher acting cold and impersonal
- Too much noise and disorder

Using a long block as a bulldozer for pushing the other blocks over to the shelves

Having a "bucket brigade" line-up of children to hand the blocks over to a child at the shelves

Filling "fire buckets" with blocks and carrying them over to the shelves to "put out the fire"

Having "construction workers" in hard hats carry blocks to shelves in buckets

Seeing how many blocks can be put back before the music record ends

Sing a song "We're picking up the blocks" (tune: *Farmer in the Dell*) as children and *teacher* do it

Make up a game about feeding the hungry dinosaur (shelves) with bones (blocks)

FIGURE 42–2   Block Pick-Up Games.

can't go outside to play until every block is put back on the shelves!" Instead, the teacher can use any number of the exciting block pick-up games listed in Figure 42–2.

- Any uncomfortable situation can be made into a fun activity for children if teachers use their creativity instead of threats or ridicule.

2. **Show respect for and acceptance of children through your communication.**

- Teachers can show acceptance by complimenting children for their language use, especially children from a non-English-speaking background. "Oh, Jorge, you said my name so clearly! I like to say your name, too."

- To help newcomers feel at ease you can play simple language games with them. "I'm thinking about a girl with new sneakers on. Can you tell me who I'm thinking about, Makayla?" "Right. Now you tell me who you're thinking about, and see if I can guess."

- Be sure to talk to children with *responsive* language that shows respect for them instead of *restrictive* language that conveys teacher control. Rather than shouting: "No yelling in the room!" you could say, "Let's speak softly." Stone (1993) reminds us:

    Responsive language is language that conveys a positive regard for children and respect for and acceptance of their individual ideas and feelings. (p. 13)

3. **Express delight and humor around children.**

- Whenever the classroom atmosphere seems gloomy or too serious, you need to insert one of your great funny ideas. How about a "funny forum," for instance? What is it? It's whatever you want to make it. Some teachers have the children sit in a circle on the floor and whisper a funny word to the child next to them, telling them to pass it along. Children can use a tissue tube for a "fun-fone." Soon everybody should be laughing.

- Or what about reading a funny book? Young children tend to laugh at certain funny words in books rather than at humorous situations. Here are several books with funny words or phrases children find hilarious:

Goodnight Moon (Brown, 1947): "a bowl full of mush."

Twist With a Burger, Jitter With a Bug (Lowery, 1995): "rumba if you wanna in your underpants."

Here Come the Aliens (McNaughton, 1995): "he's sort of gaseous and he's smelly; he has an eyeball on his belly."

Trout, Trout, Trout (Sayre, 2004): "Threespine Stickleback; Shovelnose Sturgeon; Spoonhead Sculpin; Frecklebelly Madtom"

This boy loves the "So-High-Reach-for-the-Sky" game this teacher invented.

- Teachers can make up their own games to get the children laughing. Use rhyming words and funny phrases that make them giggle.

4. Soundproof the room.

- Teachers understand that busy young children are often a noisy bunch, yet they can't keep telling them to be quiet all the time. On the other hand, living in a noisy environment for too many hours makes everyone feel stressed-out. One way to cut down on the noise is to soundproof the room. Installing ceiling tiles helps if you have the authority to do it. Easier still is putting area rugs on the floor, draperies at the windows and on the walls, and cloth of all kinds everywhere. Burlap, flannel, and rumply cloth absorb sound especially well. Cover the bulletin board with colored burlap or have a cork bulletin board. Make your job chart out of cloth with pockets for the job cards. Fasten cloth curtains to the backs of room dividers. Bring in colorful couch and floor pillows for the book center. Have rug wall hangings. Soon the children should be able to hear well and talk without shouting. As the American Academy of Pediatrics (2002) points out:

> For those with normal hearing, the stressful effects of noise will, at minimum, precipitate other stress factors present in the facility. Exposure to excessive levels of noise may have adverse physiological effects, such as increasing blood pressure. Uncontrolled noise will continually force the caregiver to speak at levels above those normally used for conversation and may increase the risk of throat irritation. (p. 205)

REFERENCES AND SUGGESTED READINGS

American Academy of Pediatrics. (2002). *Caring for our children: National health and safety performance standards; guidelines for out-of-home child care programs.* Elk Grove Village, IL: Author.

Beaty, J. J. (2004). *Skills for preschool teachers* (7th ed.). Upper Saddle River, NJ: Merrill/Prentice Hall.

Klenk, L. (2001). Playing with literacy in preschool classrooms. *Childhood Education 77*(3), 150–157.

Random House. (1999). *Random House Webster's College Dictionary.* New York: Author.

Rushton, S. P. (2001). Applying brain research to create developmentally appropriate learning environments. *Young Children, 56*(5), 76–82.

Stanford, B. H. (2001). Experienced teachers: Seeing children whole, in B. H. Stanford & K. Yamamoto (Eds.), *Children and stress.* Olney, MD: Association for Childhood Education International.

Stone, J. (1993). Caregiver and teacher language—Responsive or restrictive? *Young Children, 48*(4), 12–18.

Children's Books

Brown, M. W. (1947). *Goodnight moon.* New York: Scholastic.

Lowery, L. (1995). *Twist with a burger, jitter with a bug.* Boston: Houghton Mifflin.*

McNaughton, C. (1995). *Here come the aliens.* Cambridge, MA: Candlewick Press.

Sayre, A. P. (2004). *Trout, Trout, Trout.* Chanhassen, MN: NorthWord Press.

———

*multicultural

43 TANTRUMS

CONCEPT

Although they are rare in most early childhood classrooms, temper tantrums occasionally occur, and it is important that teachers know how to deal with them. Farber and Koplow (1996) have this to say about them:

> Temper tantrums, which are part of the normal course of the young child's development, occur and are usually resolved in the context of the young child's relationship with his caregiver. A temper tantrum may be seen to represent the child's current struggle to resolve his rage at his caregiver for placing limitations on his heretofore enjoyed omnipotence. (p. 207)

Most such tantrums occur in the home environment or at least with a parent or caregiver present. But some occasionally spill over into the early childhood classroom. They tend to represent a child's uncontrollable rage because she isn't able to accomplish something, can't have something she wants, or has to do something she doesn't want to do.

The child may throw herself to the floor, crying, screaming, shrieking, or kicking. She may throw things, hit someone, or try to damage something that doesn't work. With most young children it is an infrequent buildup of frustration that suddenly boils over and is released through uncontrolled crying or screaming. A few children have discovered that having a tantrum is a method to get what they want, and they use it for this purpose.

To the other children and even the teacher, a full-blown tantrum is a frightening incident to witness. Nothing an adult can say or do to the child makes much difference when he is caught in the throes of such an emotional outbrust. The child himself is often just as frightened about what is happening to him. What should a classroom teacher do?

STEPS

1. **Speak calmly to the child, telling her when she is ready, you will be there for her.**
2. **Pull the other children away and allow the tantrum to run its course.**
3. **Talk calmly with the child, trying to find out what caused the tantrum and how the child might deal with such feelings in the future.**
4. **Read and talk about books showing a child having a tantrum.**

ACTIVITIES

1. **Speak calmly to the child, telling her when she is ready, you will be there for her.**
   - Whether or not the child responds to what you say, or can even hear what you say, it is important that you make the effort to let her know you are not angry or upset, and you will help her come back to her happy self when she is ready.
   - You may need to say this to her more than once, but then walk away.

150

Sometimes lying on floor pillows or a beanbag chair can help a distraught child to calm down.

2. **Pull the other children away and allow the tantrum to run its course.**

   • The other children will be alarmed over what has happened and may want to help or approach the crying child. You need to calm them down by talking as naturally as possible and showing them you are not angry or upset. You can tell them to play in another area of the classroom, and when the crying child has finished, she will join them.

   • You will need to clear a space for the child where she is on the floor or at a table, putting away any objects that could be thrown or broken.

3. **Talk calmly with the child, trying to find out what caused the tantrum and how the child might deal with such feelings in the future.**

   • Wait until the child is able to communicate before you talk with her. Sometimes it is difficult to resume talking after a crying jag like this. She may have to communicate with head gestures at first. Talk with her about feelings: how she is feeling now, how she felt before, what made her feel that way. She may not be able to express what happened for a long time, if at all. Strong emotions like this are frightening for children, so go slow.

   • Empathize with the child, letting him know you understand that some things are hard to handle. Offer to help him find a different way of handling upset feelings. Maybe he can suggest his own way if this has happened at home. Sometimes retreating to a quiet corner, lying on a floor pillow or beanbag chair, or rocking in a rocking chair can help.

   • Avoid scolding the child. Instead, you need to help him save face and feel better about himself. After a tantrum children are often embarrassed about what happened in front of others. Playing with calming materials (see Chapter 24) may help him regain his confidence.

4. **Read and talk about books showing a child having a tantrum.**

   • At some point later you may want to read to the child or a small group of children a book about a child having a tantrum. In *When Sophie Gets Angry—Really, Really Angry* (Bang, 1999), Sophie explodes in anger when her sister takes away the gorilla doll she is playing with. She kicks, screams, and wants to smash the world. But then she goes outside and runs, and runs, and runs until the anger is all used up. How do your listeners feel about the way she handles her anger? What would they do?

   • In *Sometimes I'm Bombaloo* (Vail, 2002), Katie uses her feet and fists instead of words: kicking, hitting, and throwing things when she gets angry. She is sent to her room to think about it, but she continues to yell, hating everything and everybody as she throws her clothes out of the drawers. A pair of underpants lands on her head, making her laugh, and she comes back to being Katie again. What would your listeners do?

REFERENCES

Brazelton, T. B., & Sparrow, J. D. (2001). *Touchpoints 3 to 6: Your child's emotional and behavioral development.* Cambridge, MA: Perseus Publishing.

Farber, J., & Koplow, L. (1996). The traumatized child in preschool. In L. Koplow (Ed.), *Unsmiling faces: How preschools can heal.* New York: Teachers College Press.

Greenspan, S. (2000). *Building healthy minds.* New York: Da Capo Press.

Children's Books

Bang, M. (1999). *When Sophie gets angry—Really, really angry.* New York: The Blue Sky Press.

Vail, R. (2002). *Sometimes I'm Bombaloo.* New York: Scholastic Press.

TATTLING

CONCEPT

Why do some young children run and tell their teacher every time someone does something they consider wrong? Just as there are reasons for all of the actions children perform, so there are for this one. Many tale-tellers are merely repeating what has happened to them in their homes. Siblings have run to mother to tell her what that child has done. It is part of the blame-game: that someone is wrong and needs to be punished. Children who have been told on and punished at home often want to turn the tables on others. Hearron and Hildebrand (2005) tell us:

> Tattling is troublesome to some teachers, and children who tell on other children are often unpopular with their peers. Still, there are times when adults obviously appreciate having problems they may not have noticed brought to their attention. Adults can help these children develop more rapport with other children and to seek the teacher's attention in other ways. (p. 326)

Children who have told on siblings at home are often surprised to find that it doesn't work the same in the early childhood classroom, especially if the other person does not get punished. If these tattling children then become unpopular, you may have to talk with them privately about the problem. Tale-telling like this tends to occur as children grow older and can verbalize better. It sometimes becomes a problem with 5- and 6-year-olds (Brazelton & Sparrow, 2001, p. 387).

STEPS

1. **Respond to most tale-tellers by involving them in the solution.**
2. **Respond to jealousy-induced tattling by helping the child get along better with the other child.**
3. **Respond to attention-getting tattling by giving the child more attention.**

ACTIVITIES

1. **Respond to most tale-tellers by involving them in the solution.**
   - When teachers respond to tattling by punishing someone, these children's habits become even more ingrained. What is early childhood teacher to do? Experienced teachers say the best response is to thank the child and suggest a solution involving them (not the perpetrator), such as "Why don't you play in a different center, away from Dominick?" or "We have other nice trucks. Why don't you play with one of them?" Such a solution may not satisfy the teller at all, since he was expecting Dominick to be punished. If this continues to be your type of response, this child may not continue telling tales on others, but try to work out a solution on his own.
   - You remember from chapter 14: Fault-Finding that blame is not part of a problem and should not be part of a solution. Conflicts are not bad, but instead learning opportunities; and children are not bad, but sometimes need help in resolving conflicts.

Get down on the ground and pay special attention to two or three children at a time.

2. **Respond to jealously-induced tattling by helping the child get along better with the other child.**

   • Some tale-telling results from jealousy toward another child. In this case a child may tell the teacher what another child is doing wrong just to get him or her in trouble. Once again you can thank the child and suggest that she be the one to find a way to correct the situation. If the tattling continues, talk with the child about her feelings toward the other child. Help her to realize that the other child is not telling tales on her. Why is this? Is there a way the two can play together without conflict? How? At this point you may want to bring the other child into the discussion. Help them to find some common ground for resolving the difficulties. For some children it may mean they should play separately for awhile until a peaceful means can be worked out.

3. **Respond to attention-getting tattling by giving the child more attention.**

   • How are you to tell whether the tattling is caused by jealousy, attention-getting, or a habit learned from home? The cause is not the important aspect of the tattling. Once again it has to do with feelings: feelings about the other children or feelings about the child herself. A child who is not getting enough attention or does not feel good about herself may use tattling simply to get the teacher's attention. You can resolve this and many other classroom problems by giving special attention to this child and others who need it. Find time when children are engaged in free-choice activities, at snack time, outdoors on the playground (get down on the ground and play with two or three at a time), at lunchtime, as children begin their nap time, or as children wake up from nap. These are a few of the opportunities for private talks with these children. You might also ask them to do special chores for you.

   • Downplay the tattling. Do not make a fuss about it. Suggest how the child can resolve it on his own. But then spend extra time with this child to show how much you appreciate him and his presence in the class.

   • If the tattling persists, tell the child you would like her to look for something different in the classroom. Say that you are looking for children who are having fun. Ask the child to come and tell you when she finds a person who is having fun so you can put the name on your list and go and thank that person.

REFERENCES AND SUGGESTED READINGS

Beaty, J. J. (1995). *Converting conflicts in preschool.* Clifton Park, NY: Thomson Delmar Learning.

Brazelton, T. B., & Sparrow, J. D. (2001). *Touchpoints 3 to 6: Your child's emotional and behavioral development.* Cambridge, MA: Perseus Publishing.

Hearron, P. F., & Hildebrand, V. (2005). *Guiding young children* (7th ed.). Upper Saddle River, NJ: Merrill/Prentice Hall.

Wolfson-Steinberg, L. (2000). "Teacher! He hit me!" "She pushed me!" Where does it start? How can it stop? *Young Children, 55*(3), 38–42.

45 TEARS

CONCEPT

Tears, as we know, can express many emotions. There are tears of joy, of sadness, of anguish, of grief, of fear, and of rage. People cry when they are hurt both physically and emotionally. In adulthood it is women who cry openly more than men, but in early childhood both boys and girls express strong emotions through crying. Tears flow more freely in early childhood than later, because emotions are expressed more openly. Some children are more likely to burst into tears than others. It is not something they can control during their early years. But it is how you as a teacher respond to their crying that is important.

Are you someone who says: "You're okay, Daryl. You don't need to cry about it" or "Big boys don't cry"? If so, you may need to take a second look at tears and their purpose. Just as smiles and laughter cause the brain to release hormones that make you feel good, so crying helps to release toxins that have built up during an emotional experience. As Solter (1992) explains:

> *The purpose of emotional crying is to remove waste products from the body. Chemical toxins build up during stress and are then released in tears. Crying not only removes toxins from the body, but also reduces tension.* (p. 65)

STEPS

1. **Allow crying children to continue crying as long as they need to.**
2. **Do not be upset by the crying but show empathy for the children.**
3. **Help children to come back into themselves after the crying.**

ACTIVITIES

1. **Allow crying children to continue crying as long as they need to.**

   - Young children often cry when they get hurt physically, when they are very tired and nothing goes right, when a parent leaves and they must stay behind, when someone hurts their feelings, or when they are engaged in a conflict with another child. Teachers sometimes rush to stop the crying because it is upsetting them or others in the class. Instead, they should help the crying child find a comfortable spot (a rocking chair, floor pillow, or cozy corner) to retreat to and continue crying if he needs to. As Solter (1992) tells us: "Crying is not the hurt, but the process of becoming unhurt" (p. 66).

   - To force a crying child to stop crying is to distract her from feelings that need to be expressed and acknowledged. Crying is her way of expressing strong emotions. She needs to know that you acknowledge her feelings and allow them to be expressed this way. Telling her to stop crying makes her feel she is doing something wrong when she is only trying to "become unhurt." Repressed feelings can eventually cause health problems if toxins are not released.

You can hold an upset child until she has finished crying.

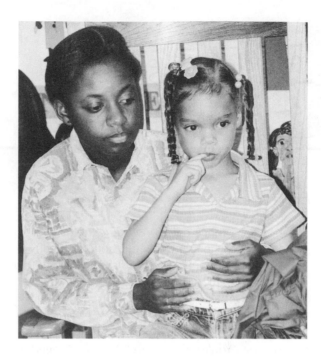

2. **Do not be upset by the crying but show empathy for the children.**

- Let crying children know you are not angry with them or upset. Some children have been punished for crying, especially outside the home when a parent may be embarrassed by the "scene" the child is making. Make sure crying children in your class know that you will not punish them for crying. Instead, help them to realize you feel bad for them and will support them in this emotional release.

- You can touch the child gently and tell her it's okay to cry and hand her a tissue. You can also hold her till she is finished crying if that will make her feel better. The motion of rocking in a rocking chair is sometimes soothing to an emotionally upset child.

3. **Help children to come back into themselves after the crying.**

- Children who have been allowed to release their feelings through tears often feel more happy and secure afterward. Give them time to recoup and then gently involve them in classroom activities again. At first they may want to play by themselves or look at a picture book. Later they may want you to read to them.

- The book *Hurty Feelings* (Lester, 2004) is an especially good one to have on hand these days when so many children are emotionally fragile. It's all about poor hippo Fragility who cries at almost every compliment her animal friends give her. When they tell her she looks nice, she flops to the ground and weeps because "nice" to her means cupcakes. Are they comparing her to a squishy cupcake? Wah! Because of her crying she loses all her friends until Rudy, the rude elephant comes along. When Rudy tries to insult her by calling her big and pudgy with legs like tree stumps, to her this means an elephant and she tells him so. This insult makes him cry, till she brings him tissues to blow his trunk. Does your formerly crying youngster laugh or cry some more?

- Talk to the children about compliments and what they can say to make someone feel good. Read the book *What Is Beautiful?* (Avery, 1995), telling what is beautiful about the person next to you and finally asking the question: What's beautiful about you? By looking into the book mirror—which is rumply—you may get some funny answers. If you don't have this book, play this game anyway with your own mirror.

- Another class used music to get children out of an upset state of mind by having everyone sing the familiar song: "If you're happy and you know it, clap your hands." They added new verses: "If you're sad and you know it, cry out loud (wah-wah)" and "If you're angry and you know it, stamp your feet (stamp, stamp).

REFERENCES AND SUGGESTED READINGS

Adams, S. K., & Baronberg, J. (2005). *Promoting positive behavior: Guidance strategies for early childhood settings.* Upper Saddle River, NJ: Merrill/Prentice Hall.

Beaty, J. J. (1999). *Prosocial guidance for the preschool child.* Upper Saddle River, NJ: Merrill/Prentice Hall.

Denham, S. A. (1998). *Emotional development in young children.* New York: The Guilford Press.

Koplow, L. (1996). If you're sad and you know it: The value of children's affects. In L. Koplow (Ed.), *Unsmiling faces: How preschools can heal.* New York: Teachers College Press.

Solter, A. (1992). Understanding tears and tantrums. *Young Children, 47*(4), 64–68.

Children's Books

Avery, M. W. (1995). *What is beautiful?* Berkeley, CA: Tricycle Press.

Lester, H. (2004). *Hurty feelings.* Boston: Houghton Mifflin.

46

TIME, USE OF

CONCEPT

Why should early childhood teachers be concerned about how they use time in the classroom? As you plan curriculum activities you know that some things take longer than others, but why should that be a guidance concern? The length of activities is not the concern. What is important are differences in children. Even children of the same age may show wide differences in abilities, interests, and needs. If these differences are not taken into account, children may express their frustration through inappropriate behavior. Some children take much longer than others to complete a project, and some may want projects to continue and not be stopped at a certain time.

Most teachers set up activities in order for children to become deeply involved in their learning. But then what happens? Do children suddenly find that time is up and they must put things away and prepare for the next scheduled activity? Do any children have problems with this? If this is true in your classroom, you may want to reconsider your use of time. A program that a number of American teachers have adopted is Italy's acclaimed Reggio Emilia approach. Lella Gandini (2002), a liaison for Reggio Children in the United States, tells us about her program:

> Time is not set by a clock, and continuity is not interrupted by the calendar. Children's own sense of time and their personal rhythm are considered in planning and carrying out activities and projects. Teachers get to know the personal time of the children and each child's particular characteristics. (p. 18)

Visitors to the Reggio schools note that there is a leisurely pace enhanced by a full-day schedule. Rather than being overwhelming to the children, it seems to provide sufficient time for being together with friends as well as for getting things done with satisfaction. Children work in small groups of two, three, four, or five that the teacher has set up so that children can communicate with one another more easily. Teachers visit groups to see what is happening and how much time is necessary for completion of tasks.

STEPS

1. **Set up your classroom in learning centers with activities designed for small groups.**
2. **Observe in the centers for several days and record how long it takes individual children to complete an activity.**

ACTIVITIES

1. **Set up your classroom in learning centers with activities designed for small groups.**
   - During the fall months one teacher took her class to a farm where apple trees grew. They were able to gather some apples from the ground and pick some from low branches. When they got back to the classroom, small groups helped to make applesauce. Another day they went out to a fruit stand and bought several kinds of apples. Then they listened to the book *Apple Farmer Annie* (Wellington, 2001) in small groups. Several activities were started.

FIGURE 46–1 Learning Centers for Apple Activities.

> Housekeeping, 6: pretend cooking; fruit stand
>
> Blocks, 5: build road from house to fruit stand
>
> Science, 2: seed project; open soaked bean seeds
>
> Math, 4: put apple counters on numbered tree mats
>
> Special art project, 4: draw apple pictures
>
> Play dough, 3: make red play dough apples
>
> Books, 4: read *Apple Farmer Annie*
>
> Cooking, 4: make applesauce

Necklaces are on hooks ready for children to select their learning center.

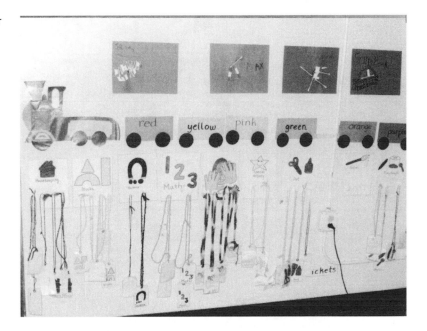

- The teacher set up her classroom for apple activities in several learning centers (Figure 46–1). Children could choose which center to work in by taking and wearing a necklace from the learning center board. The number of necklaces showed how many children could be involved in one center at a time. (See photo above.)

- These activities were continued for several days at a time as the teaching team discovered that many children could not finish their project in one day. Once everyone had made and tasted applesauce, they made fruit salad and another day sliced apples for dipping in cream cheese dip.

- More children joined the seed project when they were finished in another center and looked at bean seed "embryos" with magnifying glasses. Some planted seeds on wet sponges and watched them grow day by day. They also listened to a reading of Eric Carle's (1990) *The Tiny Seed.* Some collected apple seeds for an art project of making apple seed designs by pressing them into clay.

- The children were impressed with the different varieties and colors of apples they bought. They tried to match the real fruit with pictures in the book *How Are You Peeling? Foods with Moods* (Freymann, 1999). They drew pictures of their field trips and scribbled or dictated stories to the teachers (see Figures 46–2 and 46–3).

- Teachers made up their own activities but also obtained some materials from educational supply companies.

FIGURE 46–2 My Mommy Went to the Store and Got an Apple. My Dad Went to the Store and Got a Different Apple—a Black Apple with Blue Stripes.

FIGURE 46–3 I'm Waiting to Eat the Apples.

From Childcraft (1-800-631-5652): Science Discovery Package, "The Seasons of Arnold's Apple Tree" kit with book, plush tree with leaves, flowers, and fruit.

From Constructive Playthings (1-800-448-4115): Easy-slice plastic fruit; Soft-Sorting Food Bags with padded fabric fruits and vegetables color-coded in red, yellow, green, purple, and orange.

From Lakeshore Learning Materials (1-800-448-4456): Lakeshore Counting Boxes (10 apple tree mats and a boxful of round red apple counters).

2. **Observe in the centers for several days and record how long it takes individual children to complete an activity.**

   - Observing children involved in the various activities gave these teachers a new perspective on children and learning. The children were excited about the activities and wanted to stay with them day after day. The teachers threw out their original schedule and kept these activities going as long as there was interest. Some children wanted to start all over in the same center, which reminded the teachers that repetition is important in young children's learning. They brainstormed with the children about other apple activities they could do and came up with many new ones, including apple bean bag; bobbing for apples on Halloween; and learning about Johnny Appleseed, the pioneer apple tree planter.

REFERENCES AND SUGGESTED READINGS

Fu, V. R., Stremmel, A. J., & Hill, L. T. (2002). *Teaching and learning: Collaborative exploration of the Reggio Emilia approach.* Upper Saddle River, NJ: Merrill/Prentice Hall.

Gandini, L. (1997). Foundations of the Reggio Emilia Approach. In J. Hendrick (Ed.), *First steps toward teaching the Reggio way.* Upper Saddle River, NJ: Merrill/Prentice Hall.

Seefeldt, C., & Galper, A. (1998). *Continuing issues in early childhood education* (2nd. ed.). Upper Saddle River, NJ: Merrill/Prentice Hall.

Seefeldt, C., & Galper, A. (2002). *Active experiences for active children: Science.* Upper Saddle River, NJ: Merrill/Prentice Hall.

Children's Books

Carle, E. (1990). *A tiny seed.* New York: Simon & Schuster.

Freymann, S. (1999). *How are you peeling? Foods with moods.* New York: Scholastic.

Wellington, M. (2001). *Apple farmer Annie.* New York: Dutton Children's Books.

47 TIME-OUT

CONCEPT

"Time-out" is out. The idea that children who "misbehave" should be given time-out is an idea whose time has run out. Children who behave inappropriately need your help in ways that do not include segregating them from the others, especially in a "time-out chair." The original idea was to give them breathing time and a chance to calm down before they returned to the group. In practice, however, it was viewed by the other children as a punishment, like the old-time "dunce chair." The "dunce" was highly visible to everyone and either ridiculed or ostracized by them. In addition, the child who was set aside like this usually became even more upset, perhaps crying or thinking up ways to pay back those who put him there. As this author has noted:

> Time out, in fact, does not really help the child at all but seems instead to act as a punishment that often makes him feel more belligerent than he was to start with. In truth, time out helps only the teacher, and then only briefly, by getting the child out of the way for a moment. It is a teacher solution for a child problem. Thus a time out does not address the issues involved in the conflict nor help the child learn to deal with them. (Beaty, 1995, p. 191)

Teachers who use time-out for every little rule infraction soon learn that it fails to help. The child may calm down for the moment, but the problem is still there and the child's disruptive behavior will undoubtedly occur again. In addition, this use of time-out places a veiled threat over all the children and their actions. They soon understand that if the teacher catches a child doing something "wrong," he will be sent to time out and then have to sit in front of the whole class for everyone to see.

Should time-out, then, be totally banished as a guidance strategy? There actually is a use for removing a distraught child from the others in order to calm her down, but it should not be called "time-out" because of this term's negative connotations, and it should not be used repeatedly. Instead, the teacher can help an upset child by quietly taking her aside, talking gently to her, and staying with her until she feels calm enough to return to the class.

STEPS

1. **When an upset child needs your help to calm down, take her aside but stay with her until she calms down.**
2. **Give an upset child the opportunity to choose an activity to help her feel better.**

ACTIVITIES

1. **When an upset child needs your help to calm down, take her aside but stay with her until she calms down.**

   - The difference between time-out and taking an upset child out of the group where she has caused a commotion is that you will stay with her until she has calmed down. The other children can continue what they were doing with another staff member. As Hearron and Hildebrand (2005) point out:

> When your purpose is to help an overwrought child regain self-control, you need to stay with the child. Your calming presence conveys the message that you will help, not abandon the child to frightening, powerful emotions. This is not the same thing as rewarding the loss of control with positive attention. (p. 169)

The other children will accept your actions as necessary and supportive. They understand that you are not punishing the child but helping her to calm down. Your presence during any time-out situation makes the difference.

2. **Give an upset child the opportunity to choose an activity to help her feel better.**

   - Once she has regained her composure, talk to the child about what happened and ask her to explain it to you if she can. When she feels angry or upset like that, is there another way she can express her feelings? Would she like to finger paint what it feels like? Or paint on the easel? What about whipping up a foam of bubbles with the egg beater in a bowl of water and detergent? How about listening to a book tape as she looks through the book? Familiar picture books and tapes from Scholastic are:

     Click Clack Moo: Cows that Type (Cronin, 2000)

     Flower Garden *(Bunting, 1994)

     The Grouchy Ladybug (Carle, 1977)

     If You Give a Mouse a Cookie (Numeroff, 1985)

     Is Your Mama a Llama? (Guarino, 1991)

     Saturday Night at the Dinosaur Stomp (Shields, 1997)

     Silly Sally (Wood, 1992)

     The Very Hungry Caterpillar (Carle, 1971)

     _____

     *multicultural

   - If she chooses the book and tape activity, hopefully it will bring her back to herself with laughter, as some of these stories are quite funny—and as we know, laughter truly heals a child's hurt. Have her choose from a list of your activities, making sure there are none that would make her more upset or out-of-control. Keep an eye on her and jot down what she does and how she handles herself, for future reference.

The child can look at a book until he feels calm enough to join the group.

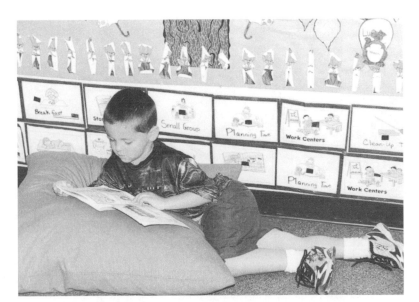

REFERENCES AND SUGGESTED READINGS

Beaty, J. J. (1995). *Converting conflicts in preschool.* Clifton Park, NY: Thomson Delmar Learning.

Beaty, J. J. (1999). *Prosocial guidance for the preschool child.* Upper Saddle River, NJ: Merrill/Prentice Hall.

Gartrell, D. (2001). Replacing time-out; Part One—Using guidance to maintain an encouraging classroom. *Young Children, 56*(6), 8–16.

Gartrell, D. (2002). Replacing time-out; Part Two—Using guidance to maintain an encouraging classroom. *Young Children, 57*(2), 36–43.

Hearron, P. F., & Hildebrand, V. (2005). *Guiding young children* (7th ed.). Upper Saddle River, NJ: Merrill/Prentice Hall.

Kemple, K. M. (2004). *Let's be friends: Peer competence and social inclusion in early childhood programs.* New York: Teachers College Press.

Children's Books

Bunting, E. (1994). *Flower garden.* San Diego: Harcourt.*

Carle, E. (1971). *The very hungry caterpillar.* New York: Crowell.

Carle, E. (1977). *The grouchy ladybug.* New York: Crowell.

Cronin, D. (2000). *Click clack moo: Cows that type.* New York: Simon & Schuster.

Guarino, D. (1991). *Is your mama a llama?* New York: Scholastic.

Numeroff, L. (1985). *If you give a mouse a cookie.* New York: Harper Collins.

Shields, C. D. (1997). *Saturday night at the dinosaur stomp.* Cambridge, MA: Candlewick.

Wood, A. (1992). *Silly Sally.* San Diego: Harcourt.

---

*multicultural

48 TURN-TAKING

CONCEPT

Learning to take turns with toys, materials, and equipment is one of the most important skills young children must learn in order to get along with their peers. For some youngsters it is also the most difficult one. Because young children are egocentric, it may seem that all of the wonderful objects in an early childhood classroom are for them alone. The fact that other children may want them at the same time has not occurred to them until someone tries to take their toy, or another child is at the easel just when they want to paint. How they are able to resolve such problems makes life in an early childhood classroom a lively and spirited experience for all concerned.

But it is an important experience. It is exactly the type of occurrence young children need in order to learn the social skills of getting along with others: of sharing, compromising, negotiating, and especially turn-taking. Your goal will be to help them resolve such problems *on their own* peacefully. The children's goal may be somewhat different. Most would like their own interest to prevail. Some will simply take what they want, even forcefully. Others may wait or simply walk away. Taking turns may not occur to them at all. The youngest may not even understand the concept. It will be up to you to introduce the idea.

STEPS

1. **Talk to the children in small groups about turn-taking when the occasion arises.**
2. **Demonstrate turn-taking with puppets or character dolls.**
3. **Read books about turn-taking.**
4. **Involve children in different turn-taking methods.**

ACTIVITIES

1. **Talk to the children in small groups about turn-taking when the occasion arises.**
   - For young children to understand a new rule or concept, explanations are best given when the situation occurs. To explain turn-taking before an incident arises makes little sense to children who don't understand it in the first place. Explaining it to the whole group at once is not as effective as talking to a small group. When children are in a total group there are always some who are not paying attention or will have no idea what you mean.
   - For instance, when two children are arguing or fighting over a toy and cannot seem to resolve the situation on their own, you can bring them together with a few other children and talk with them about how we take turns when two people want the same thing at the same time. Have the two children decide who should have the toy first and for how long. They may want to use a kitchen timer or hourglass to determine the time. Once children have become familiar with the concept of turn-taking, you may want to use the conflict conversion strategy (see chapter 6) when future difficult possession conflicts arise.

2. Demonstrate turn-taking with puppets or character dolls.

- One of the problems with turn-taking involves one child having to wait for her turn until the other child or children are finished. You can put a puppet on either hand to demonstrate a conflict over a piece of equipment that one is using. What should the waiting puppet do in the meantime? Have the children suggest. The puppet could a) stand and watch, b) do something else, c) hold the timer, or 4) wait until later to use the equipment. Adams and Wittmer (2001) find that children identify with hand puppets almost as if they were classmates.

  > Puppets can be used to role-play problems based on common classroom situations (such as name-calling, lack of sharing, or difficulty taking turns), or in response to actual conflicts. Playing out the scenario protects the identities and feelings of the children involved in the specific conflict. (p. 12)

3. Read books about turn-taking.

- *One Monkey Too Many* (Koller, 2003) is the hilarious story about what happens when there is one monkey too many to fit on a vehicle, but he won't wait and take a turn. There is room for one monkey on a bike but an extra one hops on with disastrous results. There is room for two monkeys in a golf cart but an extra one hops aboard, and they splash into a lake. A canoe for three, a restaurant table for four, and on and on, cannot contain room for one monkey too many without catastrophe. How would your listeners solve the problem?

- In *Me First* (Lester, 1992), Pinkerton the pushy pig always pushes ahead of all the other pigs until he finally learns his lesson when a voice at the beach calls out, "Who would care for a sandwich?" When he hurries to be first he finds not something to eat, but a sand witch who makes him care for her. Do your listeners think Pinkerton finally learns to take turns?

4. Involve children in different turn-taking methods.

- Once children have learned to print their names, you will be having them make all kinds of name tags for their possessions and products. Turns for special toys or games can then be chosen from children's name tags that are drawn out of a hat or bowl. Children enjoy the excitement entailed when their own name is drawn. This method works best in small groups so children don't have to wait so long.

- Children will also be able to sign up for turns on the computer, the trike, the head set and book tape, or any of the learning centers if you hang a clipboard and pencil near the spot.

This child decides to wait for her turn on the see-saw.

*Children draw names out of a
bowl for taking turns.*

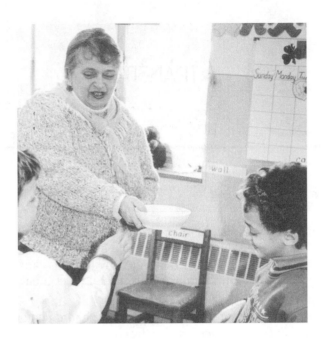

REFERENCES AND SUGGESTED READINGS

Adams, S. K., & Wittmer, D. S. (2001). "I had it first." Teaching young children to solve problems peacefully. *Childhood Education, 78*(1), 10–14.

Beaty, J. J. (1995). *Converting conflicts in preschool.* Clifton Park NY: Thomson Delmar Learning.

Bronson, M. B. (2000). Recognizing and supporting the development of self-regulation in young children. *Young children, 55*(2), 32–37.

McDevitt, T. M., & Ormrod, J. E. (2004). *Child development: Educating and working with children and adolescents.* Upper Saddle River, NJ: Merrill/Prentice Hall.

Wheeler, E. J. (2004). *Conflict resolution in early childhood.* Upper Saddle River, NJ: Merrill/Prentice Hall.

Children's Books

Koller, J. F. (2003). *One monkey too many.* Orlando, FL: Voyager Books.

Lester, H. (1992). *Me first.* Boston: Houghton Mifflin.

49 TRANSITIONS

CONCEPT

Transitions are intervals when children move from one activity to the next. By their very nature these periods of time can be upsetting for children who are deeply engaged in an activity they now must leave. If there is any amount of waiting between activities, this can also cause the more energetic children to create a disturbance. Transitions occur several times a day, opening the door for all kinds of disruption for the unwary teacher.

In too many classrooms neither the teachers nor the children enjoy the fuss and confusion of transitions. Teachers may find themselves herding the children from one activity to the next, sometimes raising their voices or making threats to accomplish this. Children may be running around and creating mischief while trying to avoid picking up and getting ready. This is not how transitions should occur in a positive guidance classroom that relies on the children as much as the teachers to help things to run smoothly.

You can eliminate many of these problems by rearranging your scheduling, eliminating unnecessary transitions, and engaging children in fun transition activities. Young children will quickly follow your lead in making such transitions enjoyable.

STEPS

1. **Minimize the number of total group transitions.**
2. **Minimize the waiting time during transitions.**
3. **Provide children with fun transition activities.**

ACTIVITIES

1. **Minimize the number of total group transitions.**

   - Look at your daily schedule. How have you arranged the activities? A list of scheduled activities in many classrooms might look like the one in Figure 49–1.
   - Rather than considering each of these activities as separate and needing a transition between them, many programs arrange their schedule in time blocks where several things happen at once, with children making choices among the activities the teachers have prepared. Figure 49–2 shows a time block schedule. Four major transitions occur between the time blocks. The amount of clock time for each block depends upon the children's involvement in their activities. Hearron & Hildebrand (2005) tell us:

     Once you have pared the number of transitions in your schedule to the essential few, you can plan to make each transition as calm and orderly as possible. This requires that each adult knows what comes next, knows what his or her responsibilities are, and be at least one step ahead of the children in the process. (p. 148)

   The children, of course, must know what comes next and what they must do, too.

FIGURE 49–1 Typical Full-Day Schedule.

1. Arrival
2. Opening circle
3. Free choice (a.m.)
4. Snack (a.m.)
5. Playground
6. Story time
7. Lunchtime
8. Nap time
9. Snack (p.m.)
10. Free choice (p.m.)
11. Closing circle
12. Departure

FIGURE 49–2 Time Block Schedule.

Block I	Arrival
	Opening circle
	Free-choice activities
	Snack
Block II	Playground
Block III	Story time
	Lunchtime
Block IV	Nap time
Block V	Free-choice activities
	Snack
	Closing circle
	Departure

2. Minimize the waiting time during transitions.

- All the activities within Block I occur as the children come in, take their outer garments off, play with toys briefly, and come to the opening circle where one of the teachers may be singing a song or doing a finger play until everyone has gathered. Circle time is brief with a greeting and hello song, and children are invited to choose their free-choice activities one by one. Snack is set up toward the end of this time block, and children are invited one by one to pick up their toys, to toilet and wash their hands, and to get their snack at the snack table. For the transition between Block I and Block II, children are chosen one by one to get ready to go out. When about half of the group has assembled by the door, one of the teachers takes them outside. As the others are ready they go out to join the rest.

- The transition between Blocks II and III takes place on the playground. The teacher has the children gather at the door and do a finger play until all are assembled. Then they go in, put their jackets in their cubbies, and sit down in the story time circle. After the story reading, children wash up for lunch by two's and three's and help to set up the tables for lunch. While waiting to be served they play a guessing game or sing a song.

- The transition between Blocks III and IV consists of each child cleaning and stacking his plate and cup, brushing teeth, toileting, hand-washing, getting out cots and blankets for nap time, and lying down. The teacher turns off the lights, turns on a gentle nap time tune, then goes around rubbing backs and whispering quietly to individuals.

- When children awaken one by one between Blocks IV and V, they can get a little toy from the nap time basket to play with on their mats till everyone is awake. Then the lights come on,

When children have to sit and wait for long, they begin thinking up mischievous things to do.

the music goes off, and children help to put away the blankets and cots. They then choose a free-choice necklace and play in one or more of the learning centers until time to depart. Snacks are put out on the snack table for individuals who want them. Finally, the teacher turns on more lively music, to which the children pick up the room and gather for the closing circle. As parents come to get them they leave the circle, put on their jackets, say goodbye until tomorrow, and depart.

3. **Provide children with fun transition activities.**

- As you see, children are kept busy during the previously described transitions with little time to wait and get into mischief. Not everyone does the same thing at the same time. But there is always time for a game, a song, or a finger play. While waiting at the lunch table for lunch to be served, the teacher may walk around behind the children saying, "Put your hands behind you and I'm going to put something in somebody's hands. Don't tell." Then the children must guess who it is. Another simple game is to hold your own hands behind your back with several fingers up. Who can guess how many? Still another game is "I'm Thinking of Someone." You say, "I'm thinking of someone with a red-and-white striped shirt on. Who is it?" Then it's the guesser's turn.

- Hilarious food stories are also fun to read while waiting for the food to come. Some are listed in Figure 49–3.

FIGURE 49–3 Funny Food Stories.

I Will Never Not Ever Eat a Tomato (Child, 2000)

Spaghetti for Susie (Coplans, 1993)

Warthogs in the Kitchen (Edwards, 1998)

Eat Up, Gemma (Hayes, 1988)*

Famous Seaweed Soup (Martin, 1993)

Mmm, Cookies! (Munsch, 2000)

Gregory, the Terrible Eater (Sharmat, 1980)

Eat Your Peas, Louise! (Snow, 1985)

Cook-a-Doodle-Doo! (Stevens & Crummel, 1999)

Bunny Cakes (Wells, 1997)

*multicultural

FIGURE 49–4   Finger Plays.

> *Down by the Station*
>
> *Eensy Weensy Spider*
>
> *Miss Mary Mack, Mack, Mack*
>
> *The Lady with the Alligator Purse*
>
> *The Wheels on the Bus*
>
> *This Old Man*
>
> *I'm a Little Teapot*
>
> *There Was an Old Lady Who Swallowed a Fly*
>
> *Where Is Thumbkin?*

- Traditional nursery songs can be sung or performed as finger plays. Everyone seems to know the finger movement for *Eensy Weensy, Spider,* but if you don't, make up your own finger plays for any of the verses in Figure 49–4.

REFERENCES AND SUGGESTED READINGS

Adams, S. K., & Baronberg, J. (2005). *Promoting positive behavior: Guidance strategies for early childhood settings.* Upper Saddle River, NJ: Merrill/Prentice Hall.

Beaty, J. J. (1999). *Prosocial guidance for the preschool child.* Upper Saddle River, NJ: Merrill/Prentice Hall.

Collins, E. N., & McGaha, C. G. (2002). Create rewarding circle time by working with toddlers, not against them. *Childhood Education, 78*(4), 194–199.

Hearron, P. F., & Hildebrand, V. (2005). *Guiding young children* (7th ed.). Upper Saddle River, NJ: Merrill/Prentice Hall.

Children's Books

Child, L. (2000). *I will never not ever eat a tomato.* Cambridge, MA: Candlewick Press.

Coplans, P. (1993). *Spaghetti for Suzy.* Boston: Houghton Mifflin.

Edwards, P. D. (1998). *Warthogs in the kitchen.* New York: Hyperion.

Hayes, S. (1988). *Eat up, Gemma.* New York: Mulberry.*

Martin, A. T. (1993). *Famous seaweed soup.* Morton Grove, IL: Whitman.

Munsch, R. (2000). *Mmm, cookies!* New York: Scholastic.*

Sharmat, M. (1980). *Gregory, the terrible eater.* New York: Scholastic.

Snow, P. (1985). *Eat your peas, Louise!* Chicago: Children's Press.

Stevens, J., & Crummel, S. S. (1999). *Cook-a-doodle-doo!* San Diego: Harcourt.

Wells, R. (1997). *Bunny cakes.* New York: Dial.

———
*multicultural

50 TRUST

CONCEPT

A child's trust in his teacher is possibly the most important achievement he or she can make in the early childhood classroom in order to control his actions and behave in harmony with others. When he first enters your classroom he may or may not trust that you will care for him, be there for him, or treat him with respect. Children who behave inappropriately in the classroom may not have developed a trusting attachment relationship at home. But school can be different from home. Children who seem to mistrust the others around them can learn to develop a secure attachment relationship with you, and this is the basis for trust. As Howes and Ritchie (2002) tell us:

> Child-teacher relationships take time to develop. First the child and teacher need to form a relationship. After the relationship is formed, it must be maintained. We found that teachers who worked to form positive relationships moved from relationship organizers to relationship partners. (p. 67)

You can start by thinking about your own relationships with others. How do you relate to those close to you? Do you trust them? Can you be open with them? Do you feel that they will be there for you in difficult times? How do you relate to first-time acquaintances? Do you feel you can trust them at the outset even when you don't know them well? If you find that your relationships with others may be on shaky grounds, you may need to rework your own strategies of relating to others before you will be successful in helping young children develop theirs.

STEPS

1. **With the youngest children you need to keep in close physical proximity to them.**
2. **With older children you need to make positive and consistent responses to their behavior and actions.**
3. **With all the children you need to treat them with the same respect you would confer on an adult.**

STEPS

1. **With the youngest children you need to keep in close physical proximity to them.**
   - Do you remember how the 3-year-olds behaved when they entered your classroom on the first day of school? They would often cling to their mothers or caregivers and then cautiously let go and venture out into the strange new environment. But they would always look back to be sure the trusted adult was still there. Eventually as they got more deeply involved in classroom activities they forgot to look back. You must serve as the trusted adult for your youngest children.
   - Help these youngsters to get involved with activities and the other children, but be right there for them when they look around. Smile or nod to them. Say a few words of encouragement. Listen closely to what they say to you. Congratulate them by name for stacking the blocks,

172

You must serve as the trusted adult for your youngest children.

using a paintbrush, playing with a doll, or lining up the little cars. Encourage them to play on their own or parallel to others until they are ready to join a group. Do not force them to participate in activities they are not ready for.

- You should spend some time each day playing with these children. One way to build a secure relationship is to use the play materials the same way the children are using them. This strategy validates the children's own efforts and demonstrates that you value their interests (Hohmann & Weikart, 2002).

2. **With older children you need to make positive and consistent responses to their behavior and actions.**
   - These children need to see that you will support what they are doing if it is consistent with classroom limits, but will intervene when their actions are unsafe or unwise. Show them that you are firm and strong in your interactions with them.
   - If their behavior becomes unruly you need to intervene calmly, talking with them about what is happening and how they can control their feelings in a more appropriate way.
   - Read them books about other children with the same control issues such as Katie in *Sometimes I'm Bombaloo* (Vail, 2002) or David in *David Gets in Trouble* (Shannon, 2002).

3. **With all the children you need to treat them with the same respect you would confer on an adult.**
   - How do you address your friends? That's what your children should be: friends. In conversations you should talk about their feelings, your feelings, your hopes for them, your concerns about them. You should share information in a personal give and take, rather than a contrived "teacher talk."
   - You should smile at them as often as possible, and laugh with them over silly things, believing that we are all human beings together in this sometimes irrational world. The fact that they are children and smaller than you and have less experience does not have to make a difference. Can't we all get along together? We can if we trust one another. If you believe this can happen, it should start with you—and them

Children need to know you will intervene when their actions are unsafe or unwise.

"I'm ready."

REFERENCES AND SUGGESTED READINGS

Hohmann, M., & Weikart, D. (2002). *Educating young children.* Ypsalanti, MI: High/Scope Press.

Howes, C., & Richie, S. (2002). *A matter of trust: Connecting teachers and learners in the early childhood classroom.* New York: Teachers College Press.

Morrison, K. L. (2004). Positive adult/child interactions: Strategies that support children's healthy development. *Dimensions of Early Education, 32*(2), 23–28.

Stone, J. (1993). Caregiver and teacher language—Responsive or restrictive? *Young Children, 48*(4), 12–18.

Children's Books

Shannon, D. (2002). *David gets in trouble.* New York: Blue Sky Press.

Vail, R. (2002). *Sometimes I'm Bombaloo.* New York: Scholastic Press.

Addresses of Educational Supply Companies

Childcraft Education Corporation
PO Box 3229
Lancaster, PA 17604
(1-800-631-5652)
www.childcraft.com

Constructive Playthings
13201 Arrington Rd.
Grandview, MO 64030
(1-800-448-4115)
www.cptoys.com

Demco Reading Enrichment
PO Box 7488
Madison, WI 53707
(1-800-356-1200)
www.demco.com

Lakeshore Learning Materials
2695 E. Dominguez St.
Carson, CA 90810
(1-800-778-4456)
www.lakeshorelearning.com

Library Video Company
PO Box 580
Wynnewood, PA 19096
(1-800-843-3620)
www.LibraryVideo.com

Scholastic, Inc.
2931 E. McCarty St.
Jefferson City, MO 65101
(1-800-724-6527)
www.scholastic.com

Weston Woods
143 Main St.
Norwalk, CT 06851
(1-800-243-5020)
www.scholastic.com/westonwoods

Other Recently Published Merrill Education/Prentice Hall Early Childhood Education Titles

Janice Beaty, *Observing Development of the Young Child,* Sixth Edition
0-13-170013-8

Jerry Bigner, *Parent-Child Relations: An Introduction to Parenting,* Seventh Edition
0–13–118429–6

Linda Edwards, *The Creative Arts: A Process Approach for Teachers and Children,* Fourth Edition
0–13–170028–6

Stephanie Feeney, Doris Christensen, and Eva Moravcik, *Who Am I in the Lives of Chidren? An Introduction to Early Childhood Education,* Seventh Edition
0–13–170996–8

Marjorie Fields and Debby Fields, *Constructive Guidance and Discipline: Preschool and Primary Education,* Fourth Edition
0–13–151256–0

Janet Gonzalez-Mena, *The Young Child in the Family and in the Community,* Fourth Edition
0–13–118921–2

Joanne Hendrick and Patricia Weissman, *The Whole Child: Developmental Education for the Early Years,* Eighth Edition
0–13–119592–1

Joan Isenberg and Mary Jalongo, *Creative Thinking and Arts-Based Learning: Preschool Through Fourth Grade,* Fourth Edition
0–13–118831–3

George S. Morrison, *Fundamentals of Early Childhood Education,* Fourth Edition
0–13–171047–8

Beverly Otto, *Language Development in Early Childhood,* Second Edition
0–13–118771–6

Carol Seefeldt and Barbara Wasik, *Early Education: Three-, Four-, and Five-Year-Olds Go to School,* Second Edition
0–13–119080–6

Carol Seefeldt and Alice Galper, *Active Experiences for Active Children: Social Studies,* Second Edition
0–13–170748–5

Carroll Tyminski, *Your Early Childhood Practicum and Student Teaching Experience: Guidelines for Success*
0–13–048817–8

Donna Wittmer and Sandra Petersen, *Infant and Toddler Development and Responsive Program Planning: A Relationship-Based Approach*
0–13–099241–0

Sue Wortham, *Early Childhood Curriculum: Developmental Bases for Learning and Teaching,* Fourth Edition
0–13–170440–0